"As engaging *and* ...
written with heart and ...
is a wonderful memoir and a great journey."

— **Susan Orlean,** author of *The Orchid Thief*

"**Married to Bhutan** is wonderfully wise and
endearing, much like the Himalayan kingdom that
is its subject. Leaming's graceful, witty prose captures
the magic of Bhutan, a place where happiness is
more than just a nice idea. It is a way of life."

— **Eric Weiner**, author of *The Geography of Bliss*

"After reading this book, I wanted to marry Bhutan—
and Linda Leaming. I was inspired by Linda's open-
hearted embrace of such a completely different culture
and way of life, take lack of plumbing as just one small
example. In the end, her book is about openness and love
and how they are expressed in the caring actions of ordinary
Bhutanese people. Linda shows us the beauty of Bhutan
and expresses a tenderness toward her earthly in-laws
that inspires me to open my own heart more and helps
me realize that we are all bigger and more capable of
love and adventure than we can imagine."

— **Cyndi Lee**, founder of OM yoga
and author of *Yoga Body, Buddha Mind*

"Paradise exists, and you can find it within the pages
of this book, which provides a delightful and charming
trek through the happiest, most beautiful, and most serene
place on earth, Bhutan. A must-read for all those who
know that the best journeys take place in multiple

MARRIED
TO
BHUTAN

MARRIED TO BHUTAN

HOW ONE WOMAN GOT LOST, SAID 'I DO', AND FOUND BLISS

LINDA LEAMING

HAY HOUSE

Australia • Canada • Hong Kong • India
South Africa • United Kingdom • United States

First published and distributed in the United Kingdom by:
Hay House UK Ltd, 292B Kensal Rd, London W10 5BE. Tel.: (44) 20 8962 1230;
Fax: (44) 20 8962 1239. www.hayhouse.co.uk

Published and distributed in the United States of America by:
Hay House, Inc., PO Box 5100, Carlsbad, CA 92018-5100. Tel.: (1) 760 431 7695 or
(800) 654 5126; Fax: (1) 760 431 6948 or (800) 650 5115. www.hayhouse.com

Published and distributed in Australia by:
Hay House Australia Ltd, 18/36 Ralph St, Alexandria NSW 2015.
Tel.: (61) 2 9669 4299; Fax: (61) 2 9669 4144. www.hayhouse.com.au

Published and distributed in the Republic of South Africa by:
Hay House SA (Pty), Ltd, PO Box 990, Witkoppen 2068. Tel./Fax: (27) 11 467 8904.
www.hayhouse.co.za

Published and distributed in India by:
Hay House Publishers India, Muskaan Complex, Plot No.3, B-2, Vasant Kunj, New
Delhi – 110 070. Tel.: (91) 11 4176 1620; Fax: (91) 11 4176 1630.
www.hayhouse.co.in

Distributed in Canada by:
Raincoast, 9050 Shaughnessy St, Vancouver, BC V6P 6E5. Tel.: (1) 604 323 7100;
Fax: (1) 604 323 2600

Design: Tricia Breidenthal

Some of the stories in this book have appeared in different form in *Ladies' Home
Journal, A Woman's Asia* (Travelers' Tales, 2005), *Tashi Delek Magazine,*
and *Nashville Lifestyles.*

Pages 56 and 138: William Stafford, "The Little Ways That Encourage Good For-
tune" and "Purifying the Language of the Tribe" from *The Way It Is: New and
Selected Poems.* Copyright © 1973, 1987 by William Stafford and the Estate of
William Stafford. Reprinted with the permission of Graywolf Press,
Minneapolis, Minnesota, www.graywolfpress.org.

The moral rights of the author have been asserted.

The author of this book does not dispense medical advice or prescribe the use of
any technique as a form of treatment for physical or medical problems without the
advice of a physician, either directly or indirectly. The intent of the author is only
to offer information of a general nature to help you in your quest for emotional
and spiritual wellbeing. In the event you use any of the information in this book
for yourself, which is your constitutional right, the author and the publisher
assume no responsibility for your actions.

A catalogue record for this book is available from the British Library.

ISBN 978-1-8485-0375-5

Printed and bound in Great Britain by CPI Bookmarque, Croydon, CR0 4TD.

For Judy Liff Barker,
for keeping the faith

CONTENTS

AUTHOR'S NOTE

All names of people and some place names have been changed as a nod to the veil of fog that often envelops Bhutan. As much as possible I've tried to update things that have changed during the almost two decades I've had associations with the country, but I also want to convey the idea of Bhutan as I see it, or saw it from the beginning. The country and its people are making tremendous changes, but the things that matter—family, culture, humor—remain. The little house on the farm where we lived outside the capital of Thimphu is still there, but the farm has become a large school.

The Bhutan I married is a rural Bhutan, full of religion, superstition, wonderful friends and family, hard work, and jaw-dropping beauty. I never use the word *pristine* anywhere else, but I do in Bhutan. Most of the people described in these pages will never read this book. My audience in Bhutan is the intelligentsia, the average resident of Thimphu: educated, savvy, and self-examining to a degree that would surprise most Westerners, but we are a little patronizing that way. For this reason, educated Bhutanese might take issue with my characterizations of life in Bhutan, my insistence that Bhutanese look at time differently and might not be punctual getting to the office. I beg their indulgence. You don't know what you have until it's gone.

I make no secret of the fact that I think my Bhutanese friends and family live more sanely than many people around the globe. They are my patient teachers. What I write and all I know is the experience of an outsider who had the extraordinary good luck to be welcomed into this unique place. It has been life-altering. In a way, it is a real marriage. For better or worse, for richer or poorer, my life belongs to Bhutan.

Just as Alice, when she walked through the looking glass, found herself in a new and whimsical world, so we, when we crossed over the Pa Chu, found ourselves as though caught up on some magic time machine fitted fantastically with a reverse. . .

— EARL OF RONALDSHAY, BRITISH GOVERNOR OF BENGAL, 1921, ON CROSSING THE RIVER (PA CHU) THAT LED HIM INTO BHUTAN

FROM THIS DAY FORWARD

Several years ago, a friend called from London about an upcoming assignment in Bhutan in March, which was only a few weeks away. He had heard nothing about his travel arrangements, agenda, housing, schedule, or fees—all he knew was that they wanted him to be there. "I can't get anyone to answer my e-mails," he said, exasperated.

"Oh," I said, trying to soothe him, "that's because the Bhutanese don't answer e-mails."

"You're joking."

"Not joking," I replied.

"I can't get anyone on the phone either."

"What month is this?" I asked. I knew it was mid-winter, but I was vague on the exact date.

There was a meaningful silence, then, "It's the second of February," he said tersely.

"You won't get anyone on the phone in February."

"Why, for God's sake? Has everyone left the country?"

"In a manner of speaking. Not much happens in the winter." I explained that government offices have a shorter workday in the winter. In November the *Je Khenpo,* the head abbot and spiritual leader of Bhutan, travels from Thimphu (pronounced Tim-POO) to his winter headquarters in Punakha (Poo-NA-ka), the next valley over, along with about 800 monks. It's an age-old custom in Bhutan and probably has something to do with the fact that Punakha is warm in winter. Besides, Bhutan is still mostly agrarian, so it's a migrating kind of place, even now. People and animals move to better pastures and better weather, where growing seasons are longer and grass is plentiful. This monk migration is the official signal that winter has arrived. It's also the unofficial nod to Bhutanese men that they can wear tights or leggings under their *ghos,* their Japanese-bathrobe-like official dress. Bhutanese are required to wear traditional dress, the gho for men and the floor-length, sarong-like *kira* for women when visiting temples or in government offices. It is a point of national pride, as well as a social leveler.

I got back around to the migrating monks. "When spring comes, around April or May, the Je Khenpo and his retinue make their way back to Thimphu and Trashichhodzong, the seat of government, and men go back to wearing nothing whatsoever under their ghos for the summer.

"They cut off an hour because it's darker earlier and cold in the offices," I said, hoping he was still with me. "That's also the reason for the tights. The cold." I heard my voice trail off.

"Okay, okay, okay, okay, O-KAY!" he said. "I don't want to hear about migrating monks wearing *tights.*" His voice had taken on a high-pitched trill. "I can

understand that there would be winter hours for government servants, especially in a mountainous country
with irregular heating. But that still leaves seven hours
in the day where they would actually be in the office.
Am I correct in that assumption?"

"Not necessarily," I ventured gingerly. "Offices open
at 9 A.M., and civil servants usually arrive on time—at
9:45 on the dot. Before that they take their children to
school and their brother-in-law to the bus station. Then
they have their morning tea break. That usually takes
about 45 minutes. Then they catch up on the goings-on
of their work mates and what happened on the latest epi-
sode of the Indian soap they all watch, and maybe they
play a little solitaire on their computers. That gets us up
to around 11:30."

"Right."

"Lunch is at 1 P.M. sharp, so they'll pop out at noon-
ish to run some errands before lunch. Maybe they have
to pay their electric bill, or get air in their tires, or pick
up their brother-in-law from the bus station and take
him somewhere else. Then they'll go home to eat or
meet friends in town at a restaurant."

"And lunch is one hour?"

"No, it's half an hour. So they get back to the office
around 2:30 or 3 P.M."

"I see."

"Right," I continued. "Then it's time for—"

"The afternoon tea break!"

"Yes!" I said enthusiastically. He was finally catching
on. "And after that it's time to call it a day."

There was silence on the other end of the line.

"They'll get in touch in their own time," I offered. My
friend said he needed to go lie down. The line went dead.

Okay, I was messing with him a little bit. But at the time—more than ten years ago—Bhutan was a sleepy, albeit magical, little place. It still is. Back then there wasn't a whole lot of urgency. But in 2006, the benevolent fourth king made a historic pronouncement. He said the people might not always have a good king. The country must become democratic. Having researched this, I can't find another instance in the history of the world where a king has voluntarily, without war or revolution, abdicated in favor of democracy. It's gotten people fired up a bit. General elections were held for the first time in 2008. Now, I'm sad to report that many people in Bhutanese offices come early and stay late.

Bhutan does seem a bit unreal at times. Hardly anybody in the U.S. knows where it is. I have friends who still think the entire country is a figment of my imagination. When I was getting ready to move here, and I told people I was going to work in Bhutan, they'd inevitably ask, "Where's Butane?"

"It's near Africa," I'd answer, to throw them off the trail. "It's where all the disposable lighters come from."

They'd nod in understanding.

So few people have heard of Bhutan. It's bad for the world, which should know that a country like it exists; but it's good for Bhutan, nestled deep in the Himalayas between Tibet and India. The tiny Buddhist country thrives with little outside influence. A modern day Shangri-La, it is one of the most seductive and interesting places on the globe.

Thimphu, the capital, sits in a bowl-shaped valley and has about 100,000 people but no traffic lights. There's no Styrofoam and few plastic bags, as decreed by the aforementioned king, an enlightened monarch who said he'd rather have Gross National Happiness than Gross National Product for his people. The army makes rum and scotch; and the government dispenses condoms—ribbed, flavored, dotted, your choice—to all of its citizens for free. The country uses two separate calendars, the Gregorian calendar alongside their own lunar calendar, which acknowledges holidays called "Blessed Rainy Day" and "The Meeting of Nine Evils." Having two calendars is an apt metaphor for how the Bhutanese conduct themselves: they are nothing if not adaptable, blending their age-old customs with life in the rest of the world. As much as the Bhutanese are modernizing, they are also taking great pains to keep their traditions. It's an ever-so-delicate balance.

ATMs have sprouted up in more than a few places around Thimphu, and now there are three banks in the country. It took a while, more than five years, for the ATMs to catch on. At first, people were lukewarm about them. Bhutan's currency came in the 1960s; before that, there was much bartering, and the Bhutanese used Indian and Tibetan currencies. There's still some bartering, and people have a healthy disregard for money. If they have it, they spend it. If they don't, they hit up a friend or relative.

The capital has its share of cars; more than 10,000 crowd the narrow streets, representing about 80 percent of the cars in the country. If you get out of Thimphu, you pretty much have the road to yourself. But watch out for the Indian Tata trucks that barrel down the narrow mountain roads, carrying nearly-out-of-date foodstuffs from India to remote villages. The bright faces painted on their hoods manage to look jaunty and menacing at the same time. If they're not loaded down with stuff, the cavernous truck beds of the Tatas traffic in human beings, serving as makeshift taxis and buses. It's not the most comfortable way to travel the winding mountain roads, which is why the trucks' sides are caked with vomit, but it's free.

You'll also find people washing their laundry in the streams beside the road, or bathing. The roads are sometimes makeshift meeting places, mating places for animals, places to sell vegetables or cheese, or places to split bamboo reeds or dry grains.

Sustenance farmers and their families make up a large share of the population; monks, including whole groups that devote their lives to praying for world peace, comprise another substantial portion of the populace. There are rich communities of flora and fauna endangered in the rest of the world, more than 480 identified varieties of edible mushrooms (said to be about one-fourth of what's actually here), and a great deal of hydro-electric power. During the summer monsoon season, Bhutan is one of the wettest places on the earth, and the country is getting rich selling electricity to India.

Bhutan is also very precarious. Because of climate change, the glaciers in the north of the country are melting rapidly. Glacier lakes are swelling and threaten to overflow their banks and burst out into the valleys where everybody lives. So along with all this peaceful beauty, there's a lot of vulnerability.

A few Internet cafés in towns like Thimphu, Paro, and Phuentsholing are thriving. There is television: local cable stations offer about 35 channels, and satellite TV is coming. Journalists who visit the country for a few days or weeks, then write in-depth articles or books, like to make much of the fact that there was no television in Bhutan until 1999, and now television and exposure to the rest of the world are corrupting the minds of the innocent Bhutanese. That's sort of true and sort of not. Many people in Bhutan had bootlegged satellite dishes and could watch television before 1999, or they had videos and DVDs and could watch movies. The average Bhutanese house with a television gets news from India, China, Korea, Japan, Germany, the U.S., and the U.K. This seems like a positive thing. And even the most isolated villager in Bhutan is surprisingly worldly, if not in the actual ways of the world, then in the ways of human beings.

There's a local television and radio station, Bhutan Broadcasting Service, or BBS, and several new radio channels have come onto the scene. Oprah is on every afternoon, as is Larry King. We have Jay Leno, David Letterman, and HBO. We watch a very popular Indian talk show called *Koffee with Karan,* with a "Lie-O-Meter" that actually pops up on the screen if Karan suspects a guest isn't coming clean. We like Indian soap operas, which are every bit as fabulous as their American cousins. There are endless episodes of shows such as *Desperate Housewives* and *American Idol,* as well as numerous reality shows and their hybrids. The current Bhutanese obsession is *Druk Star,* the homegrown Bhutanese *Idol* competition. The Indian version of *Idol* has been popular over the years, too. It had the production value of a high-school talent show, but in a country of over a billion people—many of whom have cell phones—it was an amazing spectacle. There were riots one year because the Indian equivalent of Ryan Seacrest made what was perceived to be a slur against the winner, who was of Nepali descent. The Bhutanese look down on India from their perch close to the heavens and enjoy the high drama. The effusive, emotional Indians are the Italians of Asia and make a nice contrast to the quiet, unassuming Bhutanese.

Because of geography, religion, and culture, the average Bhutanese thinks very differently than the average American. This isn't good or bad; it just is. They live at a slower pace. They have built-in bullshit detectors. They are introspective and self-examining and well versed in the geopolitics of the region in which they live. They know an impressive amount about the rest of the world. If you're smaller, you have to look outward.

Paradoxically, Bhutan, an agrarian society for centuries, has developed in isolation. Self-imposed to some extent, the isolation is also a result of geography, weather, and karma. Mountains to the north, west, and east and dense jungles in the south form natural barriers that keep the Bhutanese in and the rest of the world out. Not a lot of things or people can traverse the rugged Himalayas; there are only three very narrow ways into the country and one or two daily Druk Air flights. Buddha Air, a Nepali airline, began flights to Bhutan in August 2010 but quit the same month. Still, no other country in the world is as isolated or ethereal.

Bhutan is about as far as you can get from my family home in Nashville, exactly 12 time zones away and an epic journey that takes upwards of 36 hours to complete and requires changing planes at least four times. If you can stand the discomfort, it's worth the effort. Bhutan's lush mountains and sheltered valleys make it one of the most spectacularly unspoiled places on earth.

Even with all of the change, in Bhutan, we move at our own pace. Bhutan missed the Industrial Revolution and slept through the two world wars, and Y2K definitely came in a little fuzzy; after all, it was only the beginning of another in a long line of centuries.

The year 2007 marked the 100th anniversary of the monarchy in Bhutan. Before the monarchy, Bhutan was ruled by an elected *Druk Desi,* or regent; secular governors called *Ponlops;* and the Je Khenpo, the spiritual head of the government. But because 2007 was an inauspicious year, the anniversary was celebrated in November 2008. We just roll with time in Bhutan, squeeze or stretch it according to our needs.

The way the Bhutanese firmly refuse to be controlled by the clock is the main thing I loved about the country when I first visited in 1994. It's quirky and takes some getting used to, especially for harried, time-conscious Americans; but once you get into the swing of things, it's a great way to live. The country has worked for decades on what is unofficially known as BST—Bhutan Stretchable Time. If you have an appointment to meet someone at, say, 10 A.M., you have anywhere from an hour before to two hours after to keep the appointment. There's a very large window. It is safe to assume that the person you want to see is also running a bit late. You just sit down and wait and someone brings you a cup of tea. That you can always count on.

Before I came to Bhutan, I was always irritating friends and family in the U.S. by being a few minutes late. My mother used to say I would be late for my own funeral. ("Avoid clichés like the plague," I responded.) Americans get peevish if you're 10 minutes late, which is actually 15 minutes late because everyone gets everywhere 5 minutes early. In Bhutan, no matter what time you get there, you're right on schedule.

In fact, when making an appointment for someone to come for a meal or to fix the plumbing, a Bhutanese will say, "Come Wednesday," and that is specific enough. As long as the person shows up within the 48-hour window that is Wednesday and Thursday, everything is as it should be.

These flexible habits are age-old. Perhaps they came about because until recently—and even still, in many places in Bhutan—if there's a great distance to be traveled, it's usually on foot, so it's hard to know when you will arrive. If someone's visiting you from a neighboring village and it's late summer, he may have to stop on a mountain trail and quickly climb a tree to avoid a bear or a tiger, and that could detain him a bit. Conversely, he may show up early if the bear or tiger is chasing him. Then there's the unpleasant thought that he might never show up because he's ended up as someone's lunch. Warning: bears and tigers can climb trees, too.

In Bhutan, time is cyclical, not linear. The Bhutanese live by the seasons, which go round and round, not forward. They also believe in reincarnation, endless cycles of birth and rebirth. The way we experience time influences so many things. I think for Bhutanese, time is less about quantity than quality. They are masters of living in the moment.

I have never been someone who likes rules or structure. I don't even like ruled notebook paper. There's too much structure in the world: too much insurance, litigation, unfulfilling work, fighting; too many credit cards, receipts, forms, taxes, mortgages, traffic jams, obligations—and always enormous pressure and fear as a result.

The world lacks balance. In the U.S. we crave peace of mind; the desire for it is palpable. But we don't know how to get off what my friend calls "the hamster wheel of doom." Bhutan is good at showing people a different way to live.

I experienced my conversion, my "Aha!" moment (remember, we get Oprah, too), one morning after walking to my job. I'd been working at a little cultural school outside of Thimphu for a few months and the "commute" took 40 minutes. I could shave off an extra 5 minutes, if needed. Instead of taking the road to the forestry checkpoint, past the big prayer wheel, through the tiny village of Semtokha on the side of a hill, I could instead follow a cow path that curved up behind my house, then bore straight down through a ravine to the campus of the Royal Government of Bhutan's National Mushroom Centre, a white square block of a building with a few offices and a "mushroom production center" (a big room with recycled apple-juice bottles in rows on shelves, with sawdust and mushroom spores in them). A brisk walk across a parking lot, a hop across five stones placed strategically in a rushing brook, a climb over a two-foot concrete wall beside the latrines next to the male-student hostels of the Institute for Language and Cultural Studies, then it was a straight shot up the dirt road to Semtokha Dzong (a three-centuries-old monastery-fortress), to another cow path beside the forestry guard's house, up and then down two small ladders hand-carved out of logs leaning on either side of a barbed-wire fence, through a steep mountain meadow, past the dzong, the students' mess, and the headmaster's house to the parade ground beside the school, where we had morning assembly.

One morning I stood, as usual, in the dew-soaked grass with a handful of other teachers, waiting for the students to gather in their rows and sing the national anthem, then hear a speech and announcements by the principal. I gazed at the road that curled around the valley of Babesa about half a mile away below the school. The Wang Chu, with early-morning mist rising from its blue river waters, surrounded by farmhouses and green rice paddies, the snow-covered peaks of the Himalayan mountains above it on all sides, made me feel like I'd been transported to a page of *National Geographic*. After my purposeful, violently aerobic gauntlet of a commute, I finally felt, not like I needed to go lie down and sleep for the rest of the day—the way I had for weeks—but strong and fit, as if I could conquer the world. That or teach English to Bhutanese teenagers. The walk hadn't tired me; it had energized me. I'd traded the hamster wheel for some other kind of crazy karmic wheel. It was bliss.

I thought of other commutes back home: driving 45 minutes every morning on the interstate to get to an office and putting on makeup in the rearview mirror when the traffic slowed; being grateful that my commute took me past a Dunkin' Donuts so I could get a cup of coffee, that my car had a cup holder, and that there were no accidents to slow me down; worrying that my company was downsizing and wondering if they would keep me long enough for me to pay off the car I was driving. The radio was my shepherd, the traffic report my Bible.

I wondered what a traffic report from my commute during Bhutan's morning rush hour would sound like, and laughed. *The cow path is clean this morning. We've got Ap Khandu's cows grazing by the fly-over, so it's all clear to the Mushroom Centre with no cow patties. But you'll want to watch the mud near the boys' latrines—there could be some surprises—and be careful of that third rock as you make your hop over the brook. It's a little bit wobbly this morning.*

You find things when you're looking hard for other things. The trick is to be awake—which, granted, is harder than it seems. A sense of humor helps, as well as a willingness to accept whatever comes along—good, bad, or ferociously, violently different.

*A man met the Buddha after the
Buddha became enlightened. The man
was awed by his remarkable radiance.*

*"What are you?" the man asked. "Are you
some kind of celestial being? A god, perhaps?"*

"No," said the Buddha.

"Well, then, are you a magician or wizard?"

"No," the Buddha answered again.

"Are you a man?"

"No."

"Well, then, what are you?"

"I am awake," the Buddha replied.

LUCKY IN LOVE

In August 1994, I woke up in Punakha.

Two days in Bhutan and the rest of the world seemed like a distant dream. The beautiful, remote Himalayan valley on top of the world, with gradually sloping rice paddies and farms dotting the countryside, seemed ripe with promise.

I had stopped here for two and a half days of sightseeing on the way across the country. It was low season for tourists; and I was the only guest at the Zangtopelri Hotel, a sprawling affair on top of a mountain at the southern end of the Punakha valley, with rooms and little bungalows built around a large lobby and restaurant. It was amusing to have the entire hotel staff, which numbered about 20 men and women, focused entirely on me, so much so that I merely had to look in the direction of an empty glass at dinner and four waiters would rush the table with sloshing pitchers of water.

My trip to Bhutan was prompted by Bhutanese friends I'd met at the UN in New York in the early 1990s, who encouraged me to visit. I was planning a long trip to India and Europe, so I added two weeks in Bhutan to my itinerary. It sounded intriguing and quirky—big selling points for me to visit a place. So, in a way, it was a whim that first brought me to Bhutan. That and the fact that my Bhutanese friends were the most interesting and witty people I knew.

The hotel was cheerful and bright, built of white adobe with colorful Bhutanese iconography painted on the walls. The lobby was filled with Bhutanese treasures and weavings; it looked like a museum. The Bhutanese decorative motif is "early over-the-top"—anything will do as long as it has lots of color. If it's not colorful, it's carved. I think this is a law. Carpets and upholstery were also in the Bhutanese style—like plaid on acid. The Bhutanese are weavers, and their designs are rich and striking. I surmise how it evolved: the busy, detailed art is a wonderful counterpart to, and a nice distraction from, the austere, isolated life. The Bhutanese flair for decoration is matched only by their attention to the well-being of their guests. With impeccable, effusive manners and seemingly genuine goodwill, they make every visitor feel welcome.

There are very few people lucky enough to get to Bhutan. It's hard travel to get there, and many Westerners don't have the time. Even now, there are only 20,000 people per year who make it there, and the government requires that they travel with a guide. This helps protect Bhutan's fragile environment.

The first day, I ambitiously decided to walk the length of the valley. I had the standard-issue guide and a car and driver; but that morning I saw them sitting on the grass outside the hotel, playing cards with some of the hotel staff. I told them I wanted to walk into the valley alone; and they were positively elated, because, they said, it was the best way to see Bhutan. They grudgingly agreed to forego accompanying me so I could have this solitary experience. In a supreme act of sacrifice, they would continue playing cards until I came back.

I followed the hotel road to its intersection with the main road through the valley. Then I took the valley road past the imposing Punakha Dzong at the confluence of the Mo Chu and Po Chu—the "mother" and "father" rivers—and through to the other side of the valley. Punakha Dzong, an old fortress and monastery, sits at the mouth of the valley. It looks like 300 Japanese pagodas meeting 300 Swiss chalets, and it is so large it competes with the surrounding mountains in scale.

There are 19 principal dzongs in Bhutan, built in or around the 18th century, as fortresses and religious and government centers. They are still used today as government offices and as housing for the monks and religious leaders. The dzongs of Bhutan are full of history. When marauding hordes came down from Tibet and Mongolia, the people would hole up in the dzongs. There are vast underground stores inside them that once contained enough food to feed thousands of people from surrounding villages for months, maybe even years. Many are built over water supplies. They also have hundreds of secret temples tucked inside. Massive, sprawling, and mysterious, the dzongs are built of pounded mud, stones, and wood. They were built with no architectural plans and no nails; beams were lashed together with rope to allow for give during earthquakes. They are painted white with red roofs (the temples have gold roofs), and they look like castles—or what I suppose castles should look like in a land that time forgot.

Bhutan is suited to the leisurely pace I was setting for myself. Unlike India, where I had been traveling for about a month, here, I could let my guard down and walk. There were no beggars. The Bhutanese I met on the valley road were polite and smiling, but mostly they left me alone.

The rudimentary motor road meandered through the valley, paralleling the wide, brilliant turquoise Mo Chu, which began to flow as glacial runoff above Gasa to the north, then passed through Punakha on its way to India. All Bhutanese rivers eventually make their way into India—some, like the Brahmaputra, take a detour through Bangladesh first. The long valley curled around lush mountains terraced with bright green rice paddies. It had been raining all summer, so the vegetation looked ready to explode with emerald ripeness. Leafy, geometrical orange groves made a lovely counterpoint to unruly red poinsettia trees. Farmhouses and the occasional royal palace, all painted with the distinctive iconography, dotted the fields. Gold-roofed Buddhist temples, which you see all over Bhutan, sat high up in the mountains above the farmland. The air was delicious, clean, and sweet smelling. I felt light-headed and giddy. It could have been the altitude, or the onset of dengue fever, or bliss.

Children stopped their playing to watch and wave to me shyly, but with obvious delight, as I passed by the occasional house at the side of the road. The bravest of the children, one boy, stood as if at attention and said, "Hello, Englishman!" incorrectly judging both my nationality and my sex. I smiled, said hello, and threw in a wave. He smiled and waved back, rewarded for his effort. I was surely the most interesting thing to have come down the road in a while.

As if on cue, a herd of cows meandered past on their way to the other end of the valley. A strong smell of grass and excrement wafted around them. Some wore bells around their necks that clanged rhythmically as they walked. I let my mind drift, imagining being a cowherd in this obscure Himalayan valley. Or even a cow. It didn't seem bad.

Two hours into my walk, the valley walls on either side of the road had become steeper, the mountains more imposing. It had been some time since I had seen people or cows. The combination of high altitude and exercise had made me very hungry. Although the scenery was still breathtaking, it was clear that I should turn around and go back to the hotel and the lunch that would surely be waiting for me.

Before I turned back, I went down to the river's edge, which was about 50 feet to the right of the narrow road. There the Mo Chu was wide but shallow, with clear water flowing over smooth brown stones. I had heard it rushing beside me all the time I was walking. I took my shoes and socks off and rolled my pants to my knees. I'd just dip my feet in the icy-cold water. It would be something to tell my grandchildren if I ever had any. I inched my toes into the startling wet; and just as I thought how slippery the stones were and how I should be careful not to fall, I fell.

I laughed and pulled myself out of the water. When I put weight on my left foot, a sharp pain went up my leg. I quit laughing. I sat on the riverbank and examined my foot. I'd twisted my ankle, not badly; but I could feel heat, and it was already starting to swell. The thought of walking all the way back to the hotel, including the last 20 minutes up a mountain, made me wince. My walk had taken an unpleasant turn.

As I struggled to put on my socks and shoes, I tried to keep calm and upbeat by thinking of worse predicaments I'd been in. Unfortunately, I couldn't come up with any. Getting hurt or sick is what every woman traveling alone dreads, and until now I'd successfully avoided it. With enormous effort I got my boots on. The support of the boot on the bad ankle made it feel a little better. *This is not so bad,* I thought. But it was.

I made it back to the road. There were no cars, trucks, people, or even dogs, and there were always dogs around in Bhutan. Where was everybody? I limped along, dragging my injured foot, telling myself that it would be okay. I wasn't lost. Eventually the people at the hotel would come looking for me because I was all they had. If I could just get down the road a little bit, maybe I could find a car, a truck, a tractor, something mobile to give me a lift.

But soon the pain became my focal point. Fully miserable, I had to stop and rest after a short distance. I sat on a rock at the side of the road near a small temple that was partially obscured by an enormous boulder.

I don't know how long I sat there, but it became clear that no one was coming. So I made myself get up and start walking again. Almost at once, I heard the sound of a motorcycle behind me. I put my arm out and scooped the air like I'd seen hitchhikers do in Bhutan. A man wearing a gho and a black helmet with a visor passed me slowly. He didn't even glance in my direction. I felt panicked.

Then, a few yards down the road, he swung the motorcycle around and came back. "Where going?" he said. Most people in Bhutan speak some form of English.

I hobbled toward him. "Can I get on? Will you give me a lift?" He didn't reply. Too many questions. "Please let me get on," I said as I positioned my good leg to take my full weight and swung my bad leg over the back of the bike. I couldn't let him get away.

He turned his head sideways and said again, "Where going?"

"The hotel on the mountain," I said and pointed up. "Zang-toe-PEL-ri."

He let out a big laugh.

I learned later that Zangtopelri, besides being the name of my hotel, is the heavenly abode of Guru Rinpoche, a great Buddhist subduer of demons, a high holy man, and the patron saint of Bhutan, who brought his own brand of Tantric Buddhism to the region in the 8th century. I was pointing toward the sky and telling him I wanted to go to heaven. No wonder he laughed.

It did feel like I was going to heaven on the back of the bike. I was thrilled to be off my ankle and riding in the open air. It was my lucky day. This kind man, this wonderful man, had rescued me. He drove expertly, avoiding potholes and bumps, and he even slowed down as we passed the house with children playing outside. For all I knew, they were his children. They were pushing a small boy in a cardboard box around the yard. They looked up and, seeing me again, this time on the back of a motorcycle, shrieked with pleasure.

One little girl called out, "Hello, my darling!" as she waved furiously. They all giggled and waved and smiled elated, whole-face smiles. And I did, too, as I waved wildly with one hand and held the back of the man's gho with the other.

When we got to the hotel, I hobbled off the bike and asked, "How can I thank you? Will you come in and have tea?"

"Me jhu. Me jhu," he said. *No, thanks. No, thanks.*

I didn't want him to leave. I didn't want this dramatic rescue to end so abruptly. "Let me give you lunch."

He shook his head. He didn't want any lunch. I dug in my pants pocket and pulled out a wadded 500-*ngultrum* note. It was not an insubstantial sum—about $15 at the time—and probably more money than he would have made in a week. It wasn't enough.

"Wait! Wait!" I cried to him, hobbling toward the front door of the hotel. "Stay!" I put my hand out in the universal gesture. Two men from the staff ran down the hotel steps toward me.

"Do you have any money?" I asked them. "I'll pay you back!" They both looked alarmed. "I'm okay," I said. "This man gave me a lift."

One of them dug deep into the front of his gho and pulled out a wad of bills.

"How much?" he asked.

"All of it," I replied and grabbed it. I hobbled back to the man on the bike and tried to give him the bills, which looked to be about 1,000 ngultrum. He was still wearing the helmet with the black visor, so I couldn't see his face very well. But I did see him purse his mouth and tilt his head away from me ever so slightly, as if he was offended by my offer of filthy lucre. You have to offer things at least three times in Bhutan; it's the custom. So I offered it again, and then again. But no matter how many times I proffered it, he refused to take the money.

"He won't take it, madam," someone said.

"Thank you," I said, resigned. I put out my hand.

"Most welcome," the motorcycle man said, smiling as he shook my hand. He started his bike and drove away.

After a couple of days reading in the lobby of Guru Rinpoche's heavenly abode with my foot elevated and the hotel staff swarming around me like bees, I could walk on my ankle again.

The driver and guide took me east to Bumthang, the holiest and most beautiful valley in Bhutan. On our way, we stopped in a small town called Wangdue (pronounced Wong-DEE), and short for Wangdue Phodrang (forget it), which zigzagged over an enormous ridge with a big dzong at the top.

Outside the guesthouse where we had lunch, I saw a baby cobra slither in front of me on the path. Excited, I told my guide about it. He got a worried look on his face and bent down and pawed at the grass. "What are you doing?" I asked. "The snake is long gone."

"Looking for four-leaf clovers," he said grimly. Apparently they are a universal good-luck charm.

It seemed the snake crossing was a bad omen. Perhaps he didn't want to ride in a car with someone who had the Buddhist equivalent of the mark of the beast. I decided not to tell him that on my flight into the country I had sat next to a snake charmer with a cobra in a sack. He was part of a Rajasthani dance troupe that had come to entertain government officials and Indian diplomats during Bhutan's Indian Independence celebration. Wherever we went after that, we three, guide, driver, and I, looked for four-leaf clovers. And often we found them. The pages of my small travel diary are still full of them, pressed and dried.

After a day of hard driving over narrow mountain passes, my first view of Bumthang valley shocked me with its almost supernatural beauty. Suspended between heaven and earth, green rolling hills and expansive fields with farmhouses and temples, it seemed to go on forever. No wonder it was a sacred place to the ancients who traveled in this part of the world. If there is magic anywhere in the world, and I'm certain there is, then it is unquestionably in Bumthang.

The guesthouse in Bumthang was next door to a dilapidated little school called Chumey Primary. The parade ground, a field next to the school, looked as if it would be fertile ground for clover. The first morning, I went over and walked the perimeter of the field. There was a fresh coat of dew on the grass; and several children in their uniforms stood near the school, though it would be a while before classes began. A boy greeted me in English and asked me what I was doing.

"Looking for four-leaf clovers," I replied. Without a word, they all put down their books and pack lunches—tins tied up in bits of cloth and rope—and got down on their hands and knees. After a few minutes of fruitless searching, I glanced up to see the children standing in front of me. Each of them was holding a large bouquet of four-leaf clovers.

More children gathered, and then teachers and the principal. The students filed into rows facing a small platform and a Bhutanese flag on a pole for morning assembly. They sang a dirge-like national anthem; and then the principal gave a lecture in Dzongkha, the national language.

When assembly was over, a short, bald Indian man invited me to visit his English class. He was a friendly and engaging teacher with that Anglo-Indian clip to his voice that makes the last word in each sentence go up an octave, and he ruled his classroom with an iron fist. He asked if the students had done their homework.

"Yes, sir!" they said en masse with military precision. The children seemed to range in age from about 8 to 15, but it was hard to tell. Bhutanese children usually look younger and are smaller than their American counterparts. There were about 30 of them crowded into the tiny wooden room; and they sat on the floor cross-legged, with low benches in front of them for their books and papers. Some had no benches of their own and had to share with their neighbors.

The teacher explained that the children's homework assignment had been to draw a picture of a goat.

"What smart boy will come to the front of the class and tell us about his GOAT?" the teacher asked.

There was a frenzy of waving hands in the air and lunging toward the front of the room. The teacher selected one boy. Hands went down, resigned, and the fury stopped. At the front of the class, the boy held his picture at chest level so his classmates could see it and said in staccato, "This. Is. My. Goat. He. Is. A. White. Goat."

"Very, very GOOD," the teacher said, pleased. Then, "What smart girl will come to the front of the class and show us HER GOAT?"

From the little girls in the class came the same wild flailing of arms. The teacher selected a small girl, who came to the front of the class with her picture and held it up.

"This is my goat," she said. "He is a pink goat."

To my amazement, he sprang up from his seat. "No! No! NO!" he yelled. Flustered, he jabbed the nosepiece of his glasses violently with his forefinger and glowered down at the girl.

"You cannot have a pink GOAT! There are NO pink GOATS. There are white goats and black goats and brown goats. There are NO . . . PINK . . . GOATS! Now sit DOWN."

After the class, I chatted with the teacher. He was a good, intelligent, devoted person; but in his universe, there was no room for pink goats. There was in mine. In my classes, there would be pink goats, dancing goats, and goats driving cars. We would send goats to the moon and have them sing the national anthem. Realism was only one of many options in Bhutan.

Bhutan's charm is powerful. Like so many people who visit, I was already thinking of how I could get back.

After two weeks in Bhutan, I traveled in southern India. I stayed at the Taj Holiday Village in Goa, a resort beside the Arabian Sea. It felt like the loneliest place on earth. The late-summer monsoons had swelled the ocean so that it was enormous and gray, like the Goan sky. Just off the coastline, a massive Liberian oil tanker, the same dreary color, had run aground and sat askew and ghostly in the water. The world outside Bhutan seemed drained of color. I had never been so in love with a place and its people as I was with Bhutan. For the first time in my life, I was pining for something.

After India, I met friends in Italy. Sitting at an outdoor café at the Piazza del Duomo in Florence, I chattered nonstop about Bhutan as my two friends drank coffee, rolled their eyes, and tried to enjoy the poetic beauty of the place. I'd even gotten my film from Bhutan developed in Italy, and I made them look at the pictures.

"Don't start with the Bhutan stuff," they teased. "What about India? Weren't you in India for two months? Look around you. You're in Italy now. And you're going to France!"

"I'm going back," I said.

"Great!" they said, and offered to stuff me in a cannon and shoot me back to the Himalayas. I couldn't help myself. I was already carried away.

The Dalai Lama went up to a hot-dog vendor on the street in New York and said, "Make me one with everything."

The hot-dog vendor gave him a hot dog with all the trimmings.

The Dalai Lama handed the hot-dog vendor a 20-dollar bill. The hot-dog vendor put the bill in his pocket.

"Aren't you going to give me my change?" asked the Dalai Lama.

"Change must come from within," said the hot-dog vendor.

ENGAGED

Back in the U.S., my life took on a new focus. Everything I did was calculated to get me back to Bhutan. I told everyone I met about my desire to live and work there.

I made two long visits to the country in 1995 and 1996. I spent months traveling to every corner of the country, learning everything I could about the people and how they lived. The Bhutanese were nice about it. Some of them asked me why I loved the place so much. "Here I can be kind," I replied. And I meant it. Bhutan was teaching me things I had lost track of in the West. There was plenty of time for introspection.

"Maybe you were Bhutanese in a previous life," more than a few of them remarked, laughing. I like to think of myself as having been Bhutanese at one point. It's the only reason I can think of for my absolute passion. Many people I've met over the years who have visited are taken with the place; some return for visits or to work here for a while. Some want to return, but their lives take a different turn; their loved ones, jobs, and commitments eventually take precedence, or they get other obsessions.

From the first time I visited Bhutan until now, that has never happened to me. I remember thinking, *Are you going to be 60 years old and still trying to get to Bhutan?* And I'd answer, *Yes, I'll never stop.* The desire took over everything. It was as unavoidable as hunger. I left everyone I'd ever loved, everything I knew, my home, and everything I owned. I left my job as a freelance writer and several lucrative contracts I'd had for years. Needless to say, my family, friends, and business associates were surprised. I spent my savings and eventually sold everything I had to stay in Bhutan.

In 1997, I moved to Bhutan to teach English for no pay at a cultural school outside of Thimphu. Two years later, still as a volunteer, I was transferred to an art school in a suburb of Thimphu. I had found the center of the universe.

The other teachers at the National Art School, known locally as the Painting School, were Bhutanese *thanka* artists—makers of Buddhist scroll paintings—and wood-carvers, slate carvers, weavers, and embroiderers, who made highly refined and esoteric Buddhist art. The students were charming, earnest, and intensely focused. They devoted most of their time to drawing, painting, and praying; and they spent about two hours a day with me, learning English. They desperately wanted to converse with the few Westerners, mostly tourists, who occasionally visited the school to admire their art, so they were hungry to learn the language.

Any American who has ever taught outside the U.S. understands that when you teach in another country, there is also a lot to learn. Cultures, traditions, manners, languages—there are so many minefields, so many opportunities to make an ass of yourself. I have to say, I took every available opportunity to excel in that area. I was overwhelmed. I quickly forgot about the pink goats.

My students, who ranged in age from 8 to 23, had varying degrees of English competency. They learned a little English from me; but I learned enormous, useful, extraordinary things from them: how to drink from a water bottle without touching the lip; how to open a soft-drink bottle without an opener; how to cook a tasty meal with only a radish, an onion, and a little rice; how to keep your shoes and the hem of your kira (the Bhutanese women's traditional dress, an ankle-length piece of fabric wrapped around the body) clean when walking through mud; how to be gracious and generous when you have nothing; how to wash your entire body with half a bucket of water; how to clean the stones out of lentils; how to go to the toilet without toilet paper—or a toilet; how to stay warm on a cold night when there aren't enough blankets; how to get rid of a stye; how to stop a colicky baby from crying. And that was just in the first month.

The most valuable thing they taught me was that there are many ways to look at almost everything. At the school, we had no English books, very little paper, and no teaching aids, so we had to improvise. One of the activities the students loved was sitting on the floor in a circle and telling stories. I would start by introducing the characters. The next person in the circle would advance the plot, the next would add his or her twist, and so on until everyone in the circle had an opportunity to tell part of the story. There were about 20 to 30 students in my classes; and by the time the story got halfway around the circle, invariably one or more of the characters would have been killed off.

I might begin a story this way: "Karma is a poor village man who loves Sonam, the daughter of the village headman." The student next to me might say, "Sonam's father wants her to marry Leki, a rich man in the village." The next person might add, "Leki is rich, but he is a bad man, and he doesn't like Karma because he knows Sonam loves him." The story would go on until someone said, "Then Sonam and Karma walked across a bridge, fell off, and drowned in the river."

In any other culture, the story would end with the death of the main characters, but not in Bhutan. Without skipping a beat, the next student would say, "Then they are reincarnated." And the next student would say, "Sonam becomes a beautiful bird, and Karma is a horse. And this horse and this bird love each other."

My mind reeled; it is marvelous to think that death doesn't end things.

Old stuff was ripped out of my head and replaced with a different and more expansive view of the world. I doubt the students learned as much from me. Case in point: I didn't notice any enormous change in their grasp of the English language. However, my command of Dzongkha was coming along nicely. In those first years, I stumbled a lot. I wasn't a trained teacher, although I'd taught a little in the U.S. Evidently I was a better student. What I lacked in training, I like to think I made up for with enthusiasm. It was the greatest adventure of my life.

As I walked up the hill toward the school each morning, the strong smells of juniper and cedar, burned as an offering outside the house of a prosperous resident on the hill above the school, filled the air. The fragrant smoke curled up to the sky. I'd say hello or stop and chat with

Aum Tshering or Aum Tseten. Aum Tshering was a sharp-witted old crone, probably not as old as she looked owing to the lack of moisturizer and sunscreen in Bhutan, and she liked to tease. She'd invite me to come and sit for a while in her shop. If I was early for school, I would.

There were usually three or four of her friends, old men and women, a baby or two, a young girl, all participating in the national pastime: drinking tea. I was always a nice diversion for them, an American with an appalling command of Dzongkha, a modern-day Mrs. Malaprop, saying things like, "I have only been in this country for a short distance." For several months I inexplicably confused the word *uzen,* or principal, with *dopchu,* bracelet, and called our headmaster "Bracelet Jigme." He'd look at me quizzically when I spoke to him, but he never corrected me—probably because he was too polite. Maybe he figured, "What's the use?"

If the people in Aum Tshering's shop spoke any English, they didn't let on. Aum Tshering asked me questions I had learned to answer, things like, "Where are you from?" and "Do you like Bhutan?"

To that question I said, *"Na me sa me,"* which means "so much," or "infinitely," or, translated literally, "between the earth and the sky." If I was feeling a bit more poetic, I'd say, *"Nege sim Bhutan lu en, la"*—"My heart is in Bhutan." This would make them roar with laughter. I was like a trained monkey, enjoying my work, aware that I was entertaining people and not getting paid for it, but not really understanding why everyone was laughing so hard.

"Do you have a husband?" Aum Tshering always asked with a sly tone, knowing full well that I didn't. Her friends grinned, waiting to laugh at my reply. She had the universal tendency to talk loudly to people who aren't proficient in a language, as if the added volume would help me understand.

"*Map me!*" I'd say, looking surprised. "No husband!" I'd shake my head vigorously, eyes wide, as if I'd recently lost 50 IQ points.

"Well, if your heart is in Bhutan, why don't you marry a nice Bhutanese man?" she'd ask, being my straight man, the voice of reason. This was my cue to look earnest and hopeful. I'd say, "You arrange a marriage for me," or "I leave the latch to my house off every night, but nobody comes."

I always had the same audience and the same material, but I still made them howl with laughter every time.

Once when I was drinking tea in Aum Tshering's shop, I noticed a bucket filled with *doma,* or betel nut, on the counter, among the one-rupee sweets. Indian rupees and Bhutanese ngultrum are interchangeable in Bhutan, and currency is often just referred to as "rupees." The Bhutanese love to chew doma, a mild stimulant. They wrap it in a leaf smeared with lime and pop the whole thing in their mouths and chew it. It's a vile habit and an acquired taste—very bitter—but it does give a slight adrenalin buzz. The combination of leaf and lime makes a red juice that stains wherever it is spat, as well as the teeth and lips and sometimes the chin, so heavy users look like they're wearing red lipstick—or like good-natured vampires. Some of my co-workers at school chewed doma and would occasionally offer it to me. I had no desire to try it until the weather got very cold. My classroom had no glass in the windows, and one day the wind was whipping in. Chewing the doma made me warm for about 15 minutes, but the taste was awful and the texture even worse. It was like chewing sawdust. I'd go to the open window and spit the red juice out onto the pavement below. I couldn't stand the thought of swallowing it. The next morning during assembly the principal asked that the person spitting doma on the sidewalk beside the school please stop. He would have been shocked to know it was the newly arrived American English teacher.

Doma is normally sold in a little four-inch-tall paper cone with five pieces for five rupees. One day, little cones of doma appeared to be made from pages of *The New Yorker*. I recognized the distinctive logo, the sans-serif headline typeface, and the high-gloss paper immediately. It's not as if there are newsstands with magazines from the U.S. on every corner. In fact, there aren't any newsstands. There are very few magazines here, and the ones that make it into the country are the Indian movie magazines and a handful of out-of-date news magazines. You might be able to find bookstores or shops in New Delhi, Calcutta, or Bangkok with American or European magazines, but the expense of trucking or flying them into Bhutan would be huge. And there are hundreds of other things (food, clothing, shelter) of more use to the Bhutanese than magazines.

People here are not traditionally big readers. Until the 1960s, when the secular school system began, only the clergy and ruling class were educated. The handful of tiny bookstores in the capital sells Buddhist dharma books, children's books, and pulp fiction, as well as classics by Dickens and Dostoyevsky that are printed in India.

However, because there were no English books at the Painting School, someone working at the UN donated a bunch of *New Yorkers*. After I read them from cover to cover, I gave them to the students. They didn't read them, but they did cut out the pictures. We made stories using the cover illustrations, cartoons, ads, and photographs. My adolescent male students were fascinated with the full-page car ads. I'd see some of these pictures pasted above the beds in their hostel. They were destined for lives of making religious art, but they all had the universal testosterone-fueled fascination with expensive toys.

I can't imagine anyone getting more use out of those *New Yorkers.* After the students finished with them, I'd put the remaining pages in a box next to the trash bin outside the school. Some rag picker sold the scraps to Aum Tshering, who used them to wrap the doma. Nothing is wasted in Bhutan.

Before we got cell phones in Bhutan, communication was rudimentary. Everyone had heavy-as-a-bowling-ball Raj-era black telephones or the '60s Princess Phones with perpetually knotted cords, designed to leap off anything they're sitting on if you attempt to dial them. Making a phone call from school was the most exhausting and mind-numbing task I have ever attempted.

I rarely made phone calls, anyway, because in Bhutan, face-to-face conversation was the preferred way to get things done. If you did call someone at his or her office, it wasn't likely you would get through. He would be in a meeting or down the hall; she would be on the line and the phone would be busy; or the phone would be out of order, the cord not plugged in, or the bill unpaid. There were no sophisticated trunk lines so that somebody could be put on hold and another line could be answered. If a group of people were having a conversation and the phone rang, no one would get up to answer it. Everyone would just keep talking. There were no answering machines then, and even now I don't know of anyone who has one. No wonder there's less stress in Bhutan.

It's difficult to articulate how little the Bhutanese are slaves to their communication equipment. In the U.S., we let the phone ring three or four times, and then we expect someone to pick it up or the answering machine to kick in. In Bhutan, it's not uncommon to call someone and let the phone ring 20 or 30 times. You finish what you're doing and take your time; then, if you want, you can answer the phone.

Taking messages is often outside the habit of office workers. Nobody is that keen to write anything down and then try to follow up on it. It's a different mind-set. Asking someone to take a message is like asking him to let you drive your car over his foot. It is met with veiled hostility or incredulity. Even if he is willing, he is unlikely to have a pencil or pen and a piece of paper at his disposal. I've thought a lot about why this might be the case, and here's what I've come up with: The rest of the world isn't as obsessed with paper and documentation as Americans are.

At the Painting School, there was only one telephone, and it sat inside a locked wooden box. The locked wooden box sat on a stool, which was inside a small closet next to the principal's office, as if it had done something terribly wrong and would be punished for a very long time. The closet door had a big, black, Indian iron padlock on it and a small slit at eye level so you could see and hear the phone. You just couldn't answer it, I often thought plaintively. The peon—I liked to call him the phone wallah—whose sole job was to answer and clean the telephone, take messages, unlock the closet and the box so we could make calls, and otherwise tend to the phone was rarely, if ever, around. I felt it lent an existential quality to life at the school, as if we were all acting in a Beckett play, our own little theater of the absurd.

One day I needed to make telephone calls to two separate offices about a pending order of books. I had heard from the main education office that the books were down in Phuentsholing in a warehouse. I needed to call someone at the local education office in Thimphu to confirm this, then I needed to call someone else to get the books delivered. I asked several of the teachers if they'd seen the phone wallah.

You would have thought I had asked for a private audience with His Majesty the King. "He's not here!" one *lopen* (teacher) said, his voice registering surprise. "He's at lunch," said another, eyeing me warily. *"Ca che be?"* Why?

"I want to use the phone!" I said, exasperated. Why in heaven's name else would I want the phone wallah?

Finally, after a couple of hours, a miracle occurred. As if he had divined my pressing need, as if I had invoked him like a deity, the phone wallah appeared. A man of about 60, he was dressed in an old school uniform, a gho that was too short for him; it fell above his knees. It was obviously a castoff from a student, a small one at that. He wore rubber flip-flops—the flip-flop, or *chappel,* is a ubiquitous style of footwear in Bhutan. He smelled like he had been drinking his lunch. When I told him I needed to use the telephone, he looked surprised. I produced a cone of doma from my pocket and gave it to him. That cheered him up.

He took the doma, dug his hand into the front of his grimy gho, and fished in his pocket for the keys. I stood there waiting, a piece of paper with two telephone numbers on it clutched like a ticket in my hand. I was resolved to wait as long as it took him to open the closet door, unlock the phone, and let me make my calls. I would see this thing to the bitter end. I really wanted the books.

The phone wallah brought out a key ring on a chain with an enormous number of keys, but he knew immediately which key unlocked the closet. He opened the door quickly, as if he did it every day, which I happened to know that he didn't.

I watched with renewed hope as he unlocked the wooden box. Maybe this would be easier than I thought. A group of students and teachers had crowded the hallway. Someone was using the phone! I held out my hand for the receiver, but he shook his head and pantomimed dialing: there were obviously rules, a protocol for phone use. It was also his job to dial.

I was more than happy to oblige. I would let him do what he was meant to do. It was a heady moment.

I thrust the piece of paper with the numbers on it under his nose. I pointed in an exaggerated way to the first number: "Two . . . two . . . two . . . one . . . five," I said. The phone wallah looked at me in distress, then shyly looked at the ground.

"Madam, he doesn't speak English," one of the students offered.

I repeated the phone number in Dzongkha: "Ne . . . ne . . . ne . . . che . . . nga."

But no. I had said it too fast! The phone wallah hovered over the ancient black handset; one finger poised over the rotary dial seemed to hang there.

"Ne," I said. Miracle! He dialed the two.

"Ne," I said again. He dialed another two.

"*Ne*," I said again. He hesitated, slammed the receiver down. He had choked. We had to start over.

"*Ne*." He did it.

"*Ne*." He did it again.

"*Ne*." He choked.

He just couldn't coordinate his hand and his brain to dial three *ne*s in succession. Drunk? Maybe. Frustratingly inept? Absolutely.

I was the unconditional manifestation of patience, and he finally was able to finish the sequence of five numbers. I heard the familiar click, click, click of the phone ringing. We appeared to be on the way to victory.

But no, not quite.

He slammed the phone down hard this time. "Engaged!" he called out. He did know some English after all. Then he whipped out his massive key ring and started to lock the phone back in the box.

"Wait, wait!" I cried. "Can you try again?" A student translated. He nodded. Of course he could try again. This time I distinctly heard the phone ringing, but he slammed it down again and said, "Engaged!"

Was he deaf, too? Undaunted, I persevered. The third time was the charm. He actually let the phone ring through to the party I was trying to reach. I heard a hello at the other end, a light at the end of this crazy tunnel. He passed the receiver to me. I was euphoric. In a few seconds I got the information I needed and thanked the person at the other end profusely, then handed the receiver back to the phone wallah. He took it from me and placed it gingerly back in its cradle, as if he didn't want to tax it further. Then he pulled a grimy rag out of his gho pocket and polished the back of the receiver.

Everyone in the hallway was beaming with pleasure. He closed the phone box and was locking it when I called out, "Wait, I need to make another call."

The student translated again. The phone wallah looked at me as if to say, "Haven't we suffered enough already?"

I kept thinking of that old joke: How many phone wallahs does it take to screw in a lightbulb?

I finally made the second call.

A few weeks later the books arrived, but I never got to use them. The "In-Charge" of the supplies, Lopen Chimi, locked them in a closet because, he said, if he didn't, the students would take them and wouldn't bring them back.

Luckily, someone from the UN sent over a new batch of *New Yorkers*.

The second year I taught, I met another teacher, Phurba Namgay, a thanka painter. The intricate process of painting scroll-like thankas, depicting images of a Buddha or other deities, hasn't changed in Bhutan in about 400 years. This painter was talented, shy, and enormously kind. He had high cheekbones that made his eyes disappear when he laughed and an innate elegance. Although I found him wildly exotic and inscrutable, there was something familiar about him. We didn't speak for many months, only nodded and smiled at each other on the stairs. But then we got to know each other, and we became good friends. Then we did the unthinkable: we got married.

Men and women in Bhutan wear traditional dress to work. For men it's the handsome knee-length robe, the gho, which crosses over itself in front and ties at the side. Excess fabric is pulled up and tucked in to form a giant pleat in back, and everything is held together with a tight, wide belt.

I wore a kira, the floor-length woven dress of Bhutanese women, cinched at the waist with a tight belt and pinned with a brooch at each shoulder. Under it I wore a silk shirt, or *wanju,* and an unstructured short jacket called a *tdego* topped it all off. If wrapped correctly, the kira forms a pleat on your right side so that walking is easier. And because the belt is very tight, the fabric makes a small pouch, called a *hemchu,* above your waist to keep your keys, pens, and other essentials.

A kira requires frequent, yet discreet, adjustment. Eventually I learned to incorporate the necessaries into my personal mythology: I'd stand up, smooth the skirt of my kira, and tuck my hand into the front to straighten the fold of the pleat and show that I was ready to get going. It's a no-nonsense gesture, like rolling up your sleeves. It means "I'm ready," or "I've had enough." It's a great gesture for teachers.

Smooth the collar of your wanju, or curl it under with your hand as you talk, and this says you are charming, coy, and girlish. You can soften what you are saying by doing this. Its equivalent in Western dress would be playing with your earring.

When you walk up the stairs, you hike your kira ever so slightly so you don't trip over it. This gesture feels quite antiquated. If you do it right, it's elegant and sexy. If you do it incorrectly, you look prim and stuffy, or, in my case, like a Western woman who's not used to wearing a long dress. The very tight, wide belts, called *kera,* which hold everything together in the gho and kira truss it all up and make you stand and sit straighter. Because the clothes are so elaborate, they call attention to the body. I often felt like I was in a production of *The Mikado*.

For Namgay and me, the language of kira and gho was our mating dance. I swooned in the mornings during assembly when he would arch his back, look over his shoulder, and feel the hem of his gho to see if his pleat was straight. When I tucked my hands into the sleeves of my tdego as we chatted, he knew I was flirting.

My husband is a Buddhist. He believes our karma brought us together, as it has before in other *samsaras*—the cycles of birth, death, and rebirth in Buddhist belief—and it will countless times again as we are born and reborn. Maybe in the next life I'll be his mother; after that, maybe he'll be my dog. It doesn't matter. What matters is that we'll find each other. He doesn't doubt this. As he often says, we both had opportunities to marry before we met each other, but we didn't take them. We waited. And I came from such a long distance, over nearly insurmountable odds. His conviction is persuasive. Now I also believe. I believe in a lot of things that seem to defy reason. In Bhutan, that's just the way it is.

It does not matter if lightning strikes from above, if the earth caves in from below, if the land and the sky crash together like mighty cymbals, if your head is ablaze, if poisonous snakes crawl on your lap, whether you have time or are busy, are hungry or well fed, happy or sad; whatever happens you should not give up.

— SHABDRUNG NGAWANG NAMGYAL, HIGH HOLY MAN, STATESMAN, MAGICIAN, WARRIOR, UNIFIER OF BHUTAN IN THE 17TH CENTURY

FOR BETTER,
FOR WORSE

A few centuries ago, when Bhutan was a tiny enclave of farmers, yak, and monks, hidden away from the rest of the world—much like it is now—with only the snow-covered Himalayas to witness the arduous but happy lives of the Bhutanese, a Tibetan holy man went around western Bhutan seducing women, drinking up everybody's liquor, eating, sleeping, defecating to excess, and generally making a nuisance of himself. Drukpa Kunley (also spelled Kuenley), known as the "Divine Madman," traveled with a little dog and gave blessings to the people by whacking them on the head with a big wooden phallus. He lived from 1455 to 1529.

Oh, and yes, he could shoot fire out of his penis and spin the member around like a helicopter blade, which enabled him to get from place to place really fast. He could do other magic, too, but this trick is by far the most noteworthy. Folklore says he spewed the fire like some kind of ejaculatory napalm to get rid of demons that made life miserable for the locals. The demons ruined crops, made women barren, and caused freak snowstorms.

The folklore of Bhutan is full of stories of Drukpa Kunley's travels and exploits. No act was taboo for him. Not even incest was off-limits. One story says that he seduced his own mother. After he hounded her for a while, she agreed to the act if he would agree to just keep quiet about it and make it quick. He said he would, but then of course he didn't. He told everyone in her village about it, claiming that he would save her by exposing her as a hypocrite. With her terrible hypocrisy out in the open, she was free to concentrate on her salvation.

Namgay has a favorite Drukpa Kunley story that involves a very accomplished painter who had created a thanka that was a masterpiece. The painter was, in Namgay's words, "very pleased with himself. Too pleased, in fact. He thought even a Buddha couldn't paint as well as he could."

Since it is customary for painters to have their work consecrated, or blessed, by a high lama, this painter asked Drukpa Kunley to consecrate this special work of art. The lama agreed to do it; and when the painter painstakingly unrolled his painting, Drukpa Kunley lifted his tunic, exposed his privates, and relieved himself all over the precious art. The moral: Get over yourself. And clean this mess up.

Drukpa Kunley told the Bhutanese that when he died he wouldn't reincarnate because living on the earth was just too tiring. But while he lived, he lived fast and hard. And what did the Bhutanese do about this terrible, nasty pervert of a Tibetan lama who refused to play by the rules? They claimed him as their own, of course, and made him their national saint. I love this about them. They understand that sins of the flesh are probably the least destructive to humankind; and things like anger, hypocrisy, jealousy, greed, and pride are much more damaging in the end. This is what Drukpa Kunley taught them.

Drukpa Kunley lived during the time of the first and second Dalai Lamas; Buddhism in the Himalayan region was subject to the superstitions and teachings of the animistic religions that came before it. As Drukpa Kunley subdued demons, he destroyed them, drove them away, or converted them to Buddhism and made them protectors of the faith. His life was a nice counterpoint to the rigidity and fundamentalism of some of the practitioners.

The first time we visited the village in Trongsa where Namgay grew up, we stopped at a large domed shrine on the side of the road, built in the Nepali style and shape, with pairs of Buddha eyes on all four sides, unusual for Bhutan. It's called Chendebji Chorten and is painted white "as the snow of a sacred mountain." Someone named Lama Shidra built it in the 19th century, purportedly to cover a spot where a demon had been subdued—which is something that happens a lot here. The shrine, or *chorten,* which is also called a *stupa* in other parts of Asia, is a structure halfway between a building and a statue, filled with religious relics and then sealed. Some chortens are big enough to walk inside; they are actually buildings. But many are small, more like sculptures, so you can't go in. The relics are important to the Drukpa Kayukpa sect of Mahayana Buddhism that thrives in these remote mountains, so the chorten is a deeply revered place. There are hundreds of chortens all over Bhutan. Namgay says that when it was being built, someone was dispatched to Tibet with the combined wealth of his village to buy relics to put inside it. After a long time he returned, and he had a foul-smelling old piece of cloth that he said was a remnant of the underpants of Drukpa Kunley.

Everyone in the village was thrilled.

Namgay said the contents of the shine are cataloged on its side, and Drukpa Kunley's underpants are listed.

The shrine with Drukpa Kunley's underpants is a metaphor for the Bhutanese: they are reverent and irreverent, pious and impious, gentle and vigorous, straightforward and complex. They're at ease with seemingly contradictory things. And they're really funny.

Even the country's development policy has a bit of whimsy. The charismatic Bhutanese king, Jigme Singye Wangchuck, said in an interview about 30 years ago, when he was still in his 20s, that he would rather have Gross National Happiness for his people than Gross National Product. This declaration made by an optimistic and exceptional young king gave rise to a plan for developing the country that often eschews economic growth in favor of things like environmental preservation, good governance, culture, and tradition. How else can one of the world's least-developed countries compete with the power and wealth of the developed world? Bhutan competes by not competing. By taking its ball and going home. The Bhutanese have foregone opportunities to make money off their considerable natural resources— lumber, water, minerals, plants, and animals—in favor of their quality of life. That alone makes it a world apart.

Another influential holy man, Padmasambhava, known affectionately as Guru Rinpoche (Precious Teacher), fled from Tibet into Bhutan a few centuries before

Drukpa Kunley. This Indian saint brought Buddhism to Bhutan in the 8th century. Like Drukpa Kunley, he was no stranger to magic. He flew to Bhutan on the back of a tiger. His consort had changed herself into one to convey him. For the trip south, Guru also changed into one of his wrathful manifestations. Dorji Drolo had red skin; three bulging eyes; and big, menacing fangs. And he was on fire. He wore a tiger-skin loincloth and a necklace of severed heads. He and his consort landed high up on the side of a cliff near Paro and what is now Taktsang Monastery.

This story is told as fact in Bhutan, not as legend or myth. The history of Bhutan is so full of similar magical accounts that the line between fact and fiction is blurred, and to the Bhutanese the distinction isn't very important or necessary or real.

Many religious and political leaders made hegira from Tibet and India to Bhutan during political upheavals in those places. For centuries Bhutan was a safe haven for them. In ancient times, Bhutan came to be partially ruled by an aristocratic class of noblemen and holy men from Tibet. After their arrival in the area, they would set up their own little fiefdoms. As in Europe, the fiefdoms often fought against each other, formed alliances, and established their own clans.

What we know of the history of Bhutan is war—harsh, brutal, and mingled with miraculous events. In my mind's eye, I see these remote mountains in ancient times in a perpetual fog; and in the forests and clearings, faceless warriors, carrying bows and swords, wear leather helmets and chain-mail armor.

At the National Museum in Paro, there are finely wrought swords and daggers, leather and metal helmets, and round black shields made of rhinoceros hide. The chain-mail armor is delicate with age. There are iron-tipped arrows that were most certainly dipped in poison to ensure that a kill would be either quick and merciful or slow and painful, depending on the enemy. There are millstones, metal pots for cooking, religious paraphernalia, and other accoutrements of the rugged and spartan life the people of ancient times led.

What truly happened we can only guess, because fires in the libraries and dzongs over the centuries burned important documents. But we know that from the time Guru Rinpoche came from Tibet in the 8th century until Shabdrung Ngawang Namgyal, the father of modern Bhutan and the one who unified the country, came in 1616, there were regional rulers and a peasant class. The whole of Bhutan has only about five wide valleys suitable for habitation. It was certainly no different centuries ago. There must have been a great deal of maneuvering and dealing and fighting for the bits of arable land in these great Himalayan valleys.

Holy men—monks and lamas—were the ones who recorded history, so the saints and prominent religious figures get plenty of ink, so to speak. Bhutan's history is a sort of cult of personalities: Guru Rinpoche, Pema Lingpa, Dorji Lingpa, Drukpa Kunley, Shabdrung Ngawang Namgyal, Jigme Namgyal—the father of the first king, Ugyen Wangchuck—all the way up to the present king—these were such larger-than-life characters that such a small country could hardly contain them.

Countless other spirits or supernatural beings live in the water and earth, and their images are seen all over Bhutan. The spirits called *naga*—Sanskrit for snakes—live everywhere. The naga predate Buddhism and are part of Bön, an ancient animistic religion. Buddhism in Bhutan is "flavored" with Bön, and the two religions have meshed nicely. Both teach respect for the earth and for all sentient beings. Naga are susceptible to pollution, so if you spoil your environment and pollute the earth, then naga will exact revenge. Before you erect a house, building, or any other structure in Bhutan, you have to do a ceremony to ask the naga permission to rearrange the earth. The Bhutanese believe that many illnesses, especially skin diseases and asthma, are caused by unhappy naga. If you're environmentally friendly, the naga will bestow wealth on you and give you good crops. They have even been known to give jewels to people they like.

Lu are water spirits that inhabit lakes. They are particularly sensitive to pollution. If the water level of a mountain lake goes down, it's an indication that the lu has moved on. People in the area can do *pujas* (a Hindi word meaning "religious ceremonies," often used in Bhutan) to try to get the lu back, but it's better to keep the lake clean in the first place. Lu are good to have around because it means the lake is clean and unspoiled. They can influence your luck in a positive way, and they are generally auspicious. They, too, sometimes give jewels, particularly big chunks of turquoise, to people they like.

Imagine you're a yak herder, living at your summer grazing grounds high up in the Himalayas near some bottomless glacier lakes. The lakes are absolutely pure, brilliant blue pools of water. The intense blue actually comes from shards of rock and crystal sediment, which are mixed in with the glacial runoff, that reflect the blue sky. One day you're walking by the lake, looking for your yak herd, and you see a blue rock, a turquoise, the size of your fist, sitting on a boulder like it was placed there, just for you. Maybe you are being rewarded by the lu. Or maybe, just maybe, walking by the lake, you see a hand holding a small purse rise up out of the middle of the lake. The purse drifts over to your outstretched hand, and when you open it, it is full of chunks of turquoise and coral.

There are many stories of treasures all over Bhutan. They could be magical relics, statues, or other sacred objects. Many of the treasures were manuscripts and teachings of the esoteric arm of the Buddhism brought to Bhutan by Guru Rinpoche. They were hidden to protect the secrets contained in them, and Guru prophesied who would find many of them, as well as when they would be found. Pema Lingpa was a 15th-century saint who found some of the 108 treasures hidden by Guru Rinpoche. *Terton* is a title that means "treasure finder."

Pema Lingpa's descendants still live in the valleys around Bumthang. It is said that some of them have 6 toes on each foot. (I knew an old woman in Semtokha with 12 toes.) The Royal Family of Bhutan can trace its lineage to Terton Pema Lingpa, a reincarnation of Guru Rinpoche, who was a Renaissance man: a poet, blacksmith, translator, singer, dancer, and high lama. He received the teachings of Guru Rinpoche through meditation and dreams and found texts about Buddhism hidden by Guru seven centuries before.

Bhutan's history is filled with these freelance holy men, and some women, who traveled around a great deal. Dorji Lingpa, in the 14th century, founded a secret sect of Buddhism. Later, Ani Palmo was turned out of a nunnery because she contracted leprosy. She wanted to make a pilgrimage to a temple near Trashigang in the east, but her strength failed her. She was so pure of spirit that, legend has it, the temple turned around and came to her.

The recorded history of Bhutan begins with Guru Rinpoche, who was invited to Bumthang by King Sindhu Raja in A.D. 762. The details of his trip were recorded retroactively, seven centuries later, by Ugyen Lingpa, the founder of an important but dwindling Buddhist sect. Guru traveled throughout Bhutan and left his footprints, handprints, and body prints everywhere—on rocks, in caves where he meditated, and at important religious sites.

Guru Rinpoche was a unifying force in Bhutan because he brought Buddhism and gave the people a common history and a common myth. Whether his superhuman feats really happened is a moot point, left for Westerners, scholars, and other misfits to mull over. The loyalty and devotion to Guru of the people of this region could not be more real.

One of the most distinctive things about Bhutan is that it was never colonized. It gives the Bhutanese a very independent streak, and it has helped them keep their culture. There aren't many places in Asia that didn't succumb to the rule of another, more opportunistic state. Nothing comes to mind, anyway. Owing to the volatile nature of the neighborhood over the centuries, this is no mean feat. The rulers of Bhutan seem to have a lot of luck on their side; and at certain crucial moments in history, they made the right alliances and avoided the wrong ones.

At the turn of the 20th century, Ugyen Wangchuck, the Ponlop of Trongsa, convinced the other regional governors of Bhutan to help the British in their bid to gain influence in Tibet, so he acted as an advisor and an arbitrator between the Tibetans and the British. It is a little-known fact that the British actually invaded Tibet in 1904. It was all part of the "Great Game," a political struggle that went on for nearly a century between

Russia and England: a clumsy rivalry to gain influence in China, Mongolia, the area now made up of the Stans, and Nepal, empire-building being the flavor of the era. Ugyen Wangchuck positioned himself as an intermediary between the British, led by Sir Francis Younghusband, and the Tibetans, of whom between 700 and 2,000 ended up being slaughtered. The Bhutanese had had a taste of the British during the Duar War at their border with India, so Ugyen Wangchuck's skillful manipulation of the situation helped him save Bhutan from being annexed by the Raj. It was also a major contributing factor to his being named the first king of Bhutan. He was coronated in 1907.

Likewise, when India gained independence from the British Raj in 1947, Bhutan was quick to sign a treaty with the newly independent country, giving it a say in guiding Bhutan's foreign policy. The irony of this is that Bhutan had no foreign policy. It was closed to foreigners, and it remained so for another 20 years. But the association has been fruitful for both countries.

Bhutan is smaller in population than most American cities—about the size of Seattle—so it is culturally cohesive. People have to cooperate in order to survive in these isolated mountains. They have developed a sort of groupthink: they look out for one another.

Although the self is important, the Bhutanese see themselves less as individuals and more as members of a community: a family, a social set, a tribe, a country. This interconnectedness gives rise to a security and comfort with themselves and the people with whom they live. They know who they are, and they are generally happy. They are part of a larger whole and are willing to give up some individual freedom to help the cause of everyone else. It's not so much political; it's just pragmatic. It seems to me that the rest of the world is looking for this kind of connectedness.

In the U.S., the opposite attitude prevails, perhaps because we started as a colony of England. The individual is paramount, and our individual rights are taught to us as children. Individuality is rewarded. There are many examples of this mind-set that we as Americans don't really see because we live in it. But as much as Americans are perplexed by Bhutan's dress code, Bhutanese are stunned by Americans' sense of individual entitlement— for example, a class-action lawsuit brought by overweight customers of an airline for having seats that wouldn't accommodate their girth. It wouldn't occur to a Bhutanese to make an airline responsible for his or her size.

It's not really fair to compare the two countries, as they are like apples and oranges. Americans think the way they do for good reasons, as do the Bhutanese. But it is important to understand that people elsewhere think differently; and being aware of this and flexible about how one thinks can alleviate some discontent and, dare I say it, even make us happier.

Bhutan is also very Buddhist. As a Buddhist country, there is a certain sense of balance, brought about in large part by a philosophy that preaches nonviolence, self-awareness, and improvement through the pursuit of inner peace. In a world that has become witness to an enormous amount of suffering caused by religious fundamentalism, terrorism, greed, corrupt governments, and environmental degradation, Buddhism provides the wisdom and balance that is so desperately needed. When things are rough on the outside, it is useful to look inside.

Walking away means
"Goodbye."

Pointing a knife at your stomach means
"Please don't say that again."

Leaning toward you means
"I love you."

Raising a finger means
"I enthusiastically agree."

"Maybe" means
"No."

"Yes" means
"Maybe."

Looking like this at you means
"You had your chance."

— WILLIAM STAFFORD, PURIFYING THE LANGUAGE OF THE TRIBE

WITH THIS WING
I THEE RED

Dzongkha (Zong-KA), the national language of Bhutan, is one of the most obscure, difficult, and useless languages in the world, from the standpoint of the number of people who actually speak it, which is about 100,000 to 150,000. Most of them also speak English, Nepali, and a smattering of other languages such as Hindi, not to mention about 200 dialects. No one outside of Bhutan speaks Dzongkha. So, of course, when I moved to Bhutan, I was desperate to learn it.

I had a little book in which I wrote words and their meanings. I could say hello, good-bye, thank you, bite me, screw you, up yours, hot monkey love, and all the other essential phrases and idiomatic expressions that enrich our lives.

I asked Palden, one of the teachers in the school where I taught, if he'd help me learn, and he agreed.

Bhutanese learn differently than Westerners. This is useful information, although I didn't find it out until well into the second year of my teaching career. That should give you some idea of the caliber of teacher I was. In fact, Bhutanese learn in the exact opposite way. The first thing they do is memorize whatever they are given. They may not understand it at all, but they commit it to memory. As a result, Bhutanese are very good at remembering things. It wasn't uncommon to walk down the hall of the school and hear two or three different classrooms of students chanting passages from textbooks at the top of their lungs.

After memorizing, they are tested, basically being asked to repeat what they memorized. The tests come from India and are standardized. Students regurgitate the information in the test and are ranked according to how accurately they respond to the questions. Only later do they "learn"—that is, absorb what they've memorized and add it to their cache of knowledge, make associations and assumptions, apply what they know, reason about it, and build on it.

In the U.S., we use the Socratic method. Teachers lecture. We ask questions. Teachers ask questions. We answer. We do this back and forth, formally and informally. That's our learning process. Things get drilled into us, but we don't necessarily memorize. Our brain doesn't really function that way; it needs lots of explanation. Then we review the material, study it, and take a test. If luck is with us, we've absorbed some information we can apply, extrapolate, and reason from; and then we do well (or not) on the test, and we can be considered to have learned (or not) something.

Learning is rather messy, whatever method you employ.

Lopen Palden (*lopen* is an honorific meaning "teacher" in Dzongkha) told me I must learn to read and write

Dzongkha, then I could learn to speak it. He recited the Bhutanese alphabet and told me to memorize it. The Bhutanese borrow Chöke, the ancient Tibetan alphabet used by the clergy, because Dzongkha doesn't have a written form of its own. *Selj'e Sumcu*, the Bhutanese name for this alphabet, means "30 characters": *ka, kha, ga, nga, ca, cha, ja, na, ta, tha, da, na, pa, pha, ba, ma, tsa, tsha, dza, wa, zsa, za, a, ya, ra, la, sha, sa, ha, ah.* That "ah" at the end, the last letter, sounds so pleasing.

Easy enough. I can probably polish off 30 letters in a couple of days, I thought. I taped Lopen saying the alphabet with my handheld tape recorder. In a very short time, I'd mastered it. *Fantastic. I'm doing this so fast. I must have natural aptitude with languages.*

Then Lopen gave me some really bad news. He told me I had to learn over 100 different attachments that go on the letters of the alphabet to change their sound. He called them consonants. This may not sound like a lot, but consider the possible permutations of 100 little attachments on 30 letters. I'm not now nor was I then a mathematician; but I knew I was headed down not only a difficult, bumpy road, but also a very long one. This would be taxing. This would be painful. *Do I really want to learn Dzongkha?* What the heck, I had a lot of time on my hands. I still sort of wanted to speak Dzongkha. So I pressed on, determined not to give up so easily.

Lopen Palden said he would teach me a trick to learn the first set of consonants, which are *key, coo, kay,* and *ko;* and each could be attached to one of the 30 members of the alphabet to create a new, unique sound. They could also be combined with other consonants to make even more sounds. You see the problem immediately. Not only are there possible combinations of alphabet and consonants *ad infinitum,* but the sounds are barely distinguishable for someone unaccustomed to hearing them. After only a few hours of trying to commit them to memory, I felt like my brain would explode like a bottle of soda that had been shaken hard. As quid pro quo, I made Lopen learn to say "Rubber baby buggy bumpers" and "Seventy-six slimy snakes slid slowly southward."

I began to think that English was a better language. Why wasn't Dzongkha sensible, like English, a language that had the wisdom to borrow heavily from other languages, that didn't exist without lifting from other languages, thereby making distinct sounds that were wildly different from one another?

Also, English wisely lacks pesky aspirations. Aspirations, for the uninitiated, are perverse features of elocution in some languages whereby a word or syllable sounds different and has different meanings depending on the place from which you utter it. I don't mean in the shower or in the car, I mean a place in your body like your diaphragm, or the back of your throat, or your nose, or the tip of your tongue, and so on. Not to put too fine a point on it, in Dzongkha, the very unassuming *la* can mean "mountain," "work," "yes," or a term of respect, depending on which organ or muscle in your body it originates from. Uttering a word from the wrong place could give the entirely wrong impression. For example, you could take a conversation about work up the side of a mountain, if you aren't careful. I think you see a little of what I was up against.

So Lopen Palden had me memorize a little ditty to help me remember the first set of four consonants. *Phew!* I thought. *Now only 96 more consonants to learn.* What's 96 times 30? Anybody?

This was the little verse he had me memorize:

Ka-gee-goo-key

Ka-shab-jew-koo

Ka-dim-bow-kay

Ka-narrow-ko

I'm sure it means something in Dzongkha the way "Ring Around the Rosie" is really a little song about the plague. But I wasn't supposed to ask what it meant. I was just supposed to memorize it. Meaning would come later. Much later.

The first syllable is the actual alphabet letter, and the ending syllable is what it becomes when you attach one of four consonants. "Key" is a little hook that goes on top of the letter. "Koo" is a hook attached to the bottom right. "Kay" is a kite tail that hangs in the air; "ko" is a little bird that sits on top of the letter.

When Bhutanese children are taught this first set of consonants, they learn a pantomime dance to remember it. Think of "I'm a Little Teapot," or "Itsy-Bitsy Spider," and the accompanying gestures that are charming when little kids do them.

Now think of a much older American woman doing a children's pantomime for large groups of normally polite Asian people, known and unknown to her, who are doubled over with laughter—at parties, in offices, in shops—and you will get an idea of how I amused throngs of Bhutanese in my desperate ploy for attention. Loneliness makes people do strange things.

But slowly I began to learn.

Repeatedly during our lessons, I asked Lopen if he

would teach me a phrase or two that I could say to the shopkeepers or at the weekend market, just a little something, the tiniest phrase that would help me communicate. Many people from the villages hadn't gone to school, so they didn't speak English. He refused. That wasn't the way it was done. He was adamant that I should first learn to read and write Dzongkha.

I wanted to learn Dzongkha the right way, truly; but I was desperate to communicate, so I started to go behind Lopen's back to learn little phrases here and there. I felt like a criminal. I covertly asked my friends and co-workers. I eavesdropped on conversations in restaurants. I appropriated snippets of conversation. I was a word pickpocket, clandestinely writing things down phonetically in my notebook.

I learned how to say, "How much is this?" which is very useful when shopping. The problem was, people answered me in Dzongkha; and I didn't know the numbers yet, so I'd just nod pleasantly and move on.

Another teacher, a lovely young Bhutanese woman who taught English at the school, befriended me. She taught me idiomatic phrases like "Are you here?" "That's just perfect," and "See how I manage?" I tried to work them into conversations. When someone gave me a serving of rice, I'd say, "That's just perfect!" even if it wasn't. When I called someone on the phone, I'd say, "Are you here?" Occasions for saying, "See how I manage?" eluded me. I so wanted to say it.

I taught her to say "Awesome," "I'll get back to you," and "Bootylicious!"

My struggle to learn the language was exacerbated because the Bhutanese are culturally and religiously programmed not to talk much. The Buddha taught his students to speak only if they had something to say. Idle chatter, the American pastime, is anti-dharma, ego-driven, and thus to be avoided. In other words, you don't toot your own horn in Bhutan.

When I first came to Bhutan, I had no car, so I got a lot of rides from strangers. Hitchhiking is common here; and if you're walking on the road, someone will always take pity on you and stop. If not, you can get a group taxi. Walking to and from school and doing my weekly shopping in the market, I was often thrown together in a car with strangers, albeit kind ones. No sooner had my butt hit the seat than I started talking—about my emotional state (I'm so excited . . . I'm so psyched . . . I'm so bummed), about the weather (It's too cold today! You think this rain will ever stop?), about my gratitude (Thanks for the lift. This is a very nice car), or to get sympathy (My left shoe is pinching my big toe. I've got a bad cut on it. Don't you hate having a cut on your foot?). In the U.S., when I took a breath, the person I was talking to would take my rhetorical question as a cue to launch into his or her own injured-foot story. In Bhutan, if I had paid attention and actually looked at the drivers, I'd have seen them wincing under my steady monologue.

I'm Southern and sort of polite and was taught not to have lulls in the conversation because they make people uncomfortable. Where I come from, it's good manners to talk. Talk, and plenty of it, is the way to go. Talk when you have something to say, but don't limit yourself. Talk, also, when you have nothing to say. We in the U.S. chat people up, vent, rant, exhort, pontificate, lecture, tweet, fill the ether with noise, and generally yak it up, nonstop, usually about ourselves.

They don't do any of this in Bhutan.

In Bhutan, saying very little is the epitome of good manners. Narcissism is not a national trait. Whole families get together for celebrations, meals, births, deaths, and parties, and there are huge gaps in the conversations. In fact, there's more not talking than talking. People sit, eat, drink, and even schmooze nonverbally. They have a self-containment that we don't have in the West. It's more than okay not to talk. People are comfortable with silence.

I believe my Bhutanese friends and family are talking without talking. They are using the gaps in the conversation to convey solitude, contentment, contemplation, happiness, or sadness. The listener is attuned to what the talker is sending out, even if the talker isn't speaking. It's conveying meaning with body language—which is something that's used a great deal in Bhutan. Once you get used to the silence, it's nice, like two amoebas in a drop of water, interacting but not talking.

Of course, there are a few things that are important to say: "Your hair is on fire." "I just saw a cobra crawl in your sleeping bag." "No, thank you, I'm horribly allergic to shellfish." And there are always exceptions to the rules. One exception to Bhutanese reticence to being drunk. Drunken Bhutanese will talk until your ears fall off bleeding.

After a time, I learned to accept a ride into town, get in the car, greet the driver and any others who might be in the vehicle with a polite nod . . . and then shut up. It made people a lot happier.

When I was learning the language, there was a Dzong-kha-English phrase book that many of the shops sold. It was a small paperback, and it came in different pastel colors: pink, green, yellow, or blue. It had very useful sections on phrases in the home, at work, at school, in a government office, in the market, and at the hospital.

I read it constantly, practiced the phrases, and memorized and used many of them. But it's a universal truth of learning a language that you can memorize ten phrases from a phrase book and then just casually look at another phrase, a phrase you don't need, don't want, and would never use, and that's the one phrase that will stick with you until you die.

The section on going to the hospital had many useful things in it. One could describe in detail whatever hurt. One could ask for medicine; find out when the doctor would be back; and describe a pain as sharp, dull, burning, or throbbing. One could also learn to say, "*Go la phu bey ma nyay*"—and that was the one that stuck in my head. It was what the doctor said before examining you: "Please take off your clothes and lie down."

For obvious reasons, it isn't a phrase one would use every day, or every night, for that matter. But it was like a song that I couldn't get out of my head.

One afternoon I was in a fabric shop in Thimphu trying to buy a *kata,* a white silk ceremonial scarf given to say good luck or congratulations in the Himalayas. It's the Buddhist equivalent of a Hallmark card; and I was buying one to present at a celebration for a minister, or *lyonpo,* who had recently been promoted. As the shopkeeper was wrapping my purchase, I turned and saw a man who worked in the Royal Civil Service, a midlevel bureaucrat, respectable and proper. He knew me because, as a foreigner living in Bhutan, I had to go to his office every time I wanted to leave Thimphu. He had to sign a piece of paper that said I could travel around the hinterlands—an annoying bit of bureaucracy for Bhutanese and foreigners alike. He was one of those people I always felt nervous and awkward around. He brought out my inner doofus.

So I was desperate to show off my new semi-command of the Bhutanese language; and I turned to look at him in order to say, "I believe you are going to the reception for Lyonpo?"

Instead, I smiled pleasantly and said, "Please take off your clothes and lie down."

I didn't realize my mistake until I saw the shocked look on his face. His eyebrow arched its disapproval; and he backed away from me and out of the shop, presumably to buy his kata elsewhere, somewhere that didn't have repulsive Americans spewing vile come-ons.

I stood there, frozen. The phrase that dared not speak its name had been unleashed. I looked at the shopkeeper on the other side of the counter. She was frozen, too, my parcel in her extended hand. Our eyes met.

"*Ya la MA!*" I said, this time appropriate to the situation: *Oh, my GOD!*

"*Embey!*" she said. *You got that right!* She started giggling. Then I laughed, too. We both laughed for what seemed like a long time.

I struggled with the language for several years, creating my own brand of pidgin Dzongkha. When Namgay and I married, it improved a little. The Bhutanese have a saying: two heads, one pillow, is the optimal way to learn a language.

One thing that works both for and against me is my fearlessness. I don't hesitate to speak if I don't know a word; I just use one that's close or that sounds like the word I want.

Once I was sitting at Namgay's sister's house during a family puja. His mother and I were on a bed, chatting and drinking tea. Of course, she doesn't know any English, so we spoke in Dzongkha. We were well into a conversation when Namgay's eight-year-old nephew, Tashi, came into the room. After a few minutes he doubled over with laughter. I asked him what was so funny. He'd been taught to be respectful, so he wouldn't tell me.

I called to Namgay and asked him why Tashi was amused. He asked Tashi; and the boy spoke rapidly between giggles, telling Namgay that he was laughing at our conversation; and then he related it to Namgay, who also started chuckling. Apparently, I had said something like, "The weather is very cold"; and my mother-in-law had said, "Yes, Paro is a beautiful valley"; and then I said, "You know, Paro is a beautiful valley"; and she said, "Yes, I will go and collect mushrooms tomorrow." We were talking over each other's heads, misinterpreting, but carrying on what we thought to be a nice conversation, neither of us the wiser. On some level I think it still qualifies as communicating.

When I go outside of Thimphu I love to talk with people in the villages. They are incredibly funny and are usually surprised to meet a foreigner who butchers their language so brazenly.

People I meet on mule trails going from one village to another are often of a certain age, 50 or older, and so have never had any formal education. The secular school system only started in the early 1960s, and many children in remote areas were needed to work on the farms. Since there weren't many schools, the children would have to leave their parents and go to boarding school. This was especially hard for girls, which is why so many grandmothers in Bhutan don't speak English.

Once on a trail going from Gangtey to Wangdue, a friend and I caught up to an old woman who was walking behind a strapping young man. The two of them were obviously together. She carried a small cloth bundle that didn't look very heavy, but he had a large burlap sack of rice on his back. It was a 50-kilogram bag, which meant he was carrying a little over 100 pounds.

I struck up a conversation with the woman, asking her what everybody in Bhutan asks when you meet on a road or forest path: *"Ca le om?"* "Where are you coming from?"

She'd been to Wangdue for shopping and now was headed home to her farm. She gestured up and to the left with her head: it was another few hours' walk, she said. Our conversation flowed because she spoke slowly; and as long as a conversation didn't veer too far away from food, body parts, and household things, I could follow along. Also, I think she might have been a little drunk, making her talk more slowly.

The old woman was entertaining. She was a woman of property; she had a little patch of land. She was also a cowherd, looking after the cows of a rich man. This gave her some status in her village, I was sure. Her kira was hand-woven, but worn; and instead of a wanju, she wore a flannel shirt underneath, maybe borrowed from the young man. The ladies of a certain age in Bhutan wear six- to eight-inch-wide woven belts slung low on their hips instead of cinching them at the waist like younger women, and they carry all manner of things in a fold in their kiras above the belt. Sometimes they have so much stuff it looks like they have giant beer bellies. My new acquaintance was no exception. She wore gold and turquoise earrings; and a *dzi,* or Tibetan bead, a highly prized and valuable cylindrical agate with a brown-and-cream geometric pattern for which the ancient formula is lost, was tied on a string around her neck. That meant she was not poor by village standards. Her hair was cut short and jet black, but many of the older people dye their hair with cheap Chinese dye that you can get all over Bhutan. And even from a distance her clothes gave off a smell of wood smoke. That is perhaps the most evocative smell of Bhutan. In the villages in winter, the smell means warmth, food, and survival. It's my favorite smell.

I gestured toward the young man. He looked like he might be her grandson, but ladies from the village, who have spent their whole lives outside in the sun without moisturizer, generally aren't as old as they look. Even accounting for sun damage, when I did some quick math in my head, there seemed to be at least a 30-year age difference between the two of them. I decided to err on the side of caution.

"Is that your son?" I asked her.

"Oh, no," she laughed. "He's my husband!"

"Really?" I tried to keep my jaw from hitting the ground.

Sure," she said. Then she leaned her head in close to mine and whispered the phrase I'd learned from my colleague at the school, the idiom I'd never been able to use: "See how I manage?"

I'm sure I looked confused. Did I hear her right?

"You heard right," she said to me in Dzongkha, as if reading my thoughts.

She wagged her head. Her merry eyes danced, and then she let out a big laugh.

Give wherever the mind feels confidence.

— SHAKYAMUNI BUDDHA

WOOING

Kawajangsa, on the edge of Thimphu, is just outside the town. It's technically a part of Thimphu, but it retains its own village heart. It is home to the National Art School and to artists and artisans from all over Bhutan.

Kawajangsa's road starts by the National Library, a perfectly proportioned four-story building, tall and clean, bright white, with elaborate painting around the eaves and windows, with the gingerbread-gone-mad look of Bhutan's elaborate architecture. The sculpture lopen of the Painting School made the enormous dragon-headed gargoyles at each of the four corners.

The library sits on the side of the road above a field and has the stately air of library buildings all over the world. It houses numerous collections of Buddhist religious texts; and each floor has a beautiful altar with statues of Buddhas, including Manjushri, the Buddha of Knowledge. There are always red-robed monks reading and studying, so it feels like a scholarly temple.

A few years ago there was a problem with bugs eating the religious texts. This presented a moral dilemma:

the religious texts were Buddhist, and each proclaimed in different ways the sanctity of all life. What were the library officials to do? Bhutan doesn't have any pest control because everyone lives in harmony with all sentient beings. They did some research and consulted experts and finally found alternative, herbal ways to slow the progress of the vermin, such as camphor, which repels but doesn't kill bugs.

Past the library, the road snakes to the right at the Seven Sisters Hotel. *Hotel* in Asia doesn't just mean "hotel"; it can also mean "restaurant" or "bar." All seven sisters are usually there with their many kids, so the place is always crowded. The road climbs up the hill to Dasho Sonam Dorji's sprawling house, which dominates a curve in the road. He was the first principal of the Painting School and is a master craftsman. His house has been added on to many times over the decades to accommodate generations of family. Just across from Sonam Dorji's, the *gup,* or mayor, of Kawajangsa is expanding his house. Instead of the traditional mud, he's building with concrete and rebar, so his house has a look of relative affluence and is all right angles. He's made room for some shops on the first floor so students at the Painting School can sell their work.

Directly behind Sonam Dorji's house is the National Heritage Museum, an unpainted three-story mud house, the oldest house in the area, which has been fixed up and fitted with baskets, bowls, beds, fabric, and other implements to show how Bhutanese people lived generations ago. It's a beautiful living museum; and the objects in the house are positioned casually but just so, as if the family who lived there has just gotten up and gone outside for a moment.

The mementos in the museum are identical to the wooden rice boxes, cupboards, looms, and other household essentials used by the inhabitants of neighboring houses in Kawajangsa today. If you walk into my sister-in-law's house next door, you'll see the same looms, gourd dippers, ancient baskets, and other household accoutrements. The only difference is that a family is there and they are actually using the stuff.

Next, the road winds to the left around a hillock on which stands the Painting School. The official name of the school is *Zorig Chusum Pekhang*, the Institute for the Thirteen Arts of Bhutan. These arts are painting, calligraphy, wood carving, embroidery, casting, leatherwork, bamboo works, blacksmithing, masonry, sculpture, pottery, gold- and silversmithing, and weaving. The school has a hundred students now; but a few years ago there were only 60 students, who lived in hostel rooms on the ground floor. Bhutan is getting younger: now almost half the 650,000 people in the country are under 15, so schools are expanding out of necessity.

All along the side of the road, there are shops and houses where teachers and their families live. There is an open-air quality to life in Bhutan. Inside or outside, there is often a breeze. Windows are never fitted, so nothing is airtight. Many windows have no screens and some have no glass. Traditional houses just have wooden shutters that are closed at night.

Many houses are constructed on the cheap, with whatever materials are at hand, like wood, stone, and mud, so they have a tumbledown look to them, and no right angles. The Thimphu valley isn't very big, so space is at a premium; the houses are all packed together, and most of them have two or three stories. Toilets are often outside, as are the water sources, though the newer houses and apartments have indoor plumbing. People visit the latrines and bring in their water for cooking and washing in buckets filled from community taps.

This patchwork of houses, small shops, offices, and "canteens"—small tearooms that sell tea, *momo* or meat dumplings, instant coffee, beer, whiskey, and soup— with an odd animal wandering along the road, a chicken, cow, or dog, gives the place a Breughelesque village atmosphere. But instead of ruddy Dutch peasants, there are beautiful, lean Bhutanese sitting on doorsteps, talking between the ground-floor windows of the houses, or washing clothes amid the waterspouts and plastic tubs. Everywhere laundry is drying, hung on lines and bushes; and those beautiful, colorful, large rectangles of Bhutanese textile that women wear as kiras flap in the breeze. Rows of colorful prayer flags hang on long poles in the yards or wave from the roofs of the houses, giving the town a carnival look and adding to the feeling of motion.

It's not unusual to see a small child in the middle of the road, happily playing with a puppy. The occasional car creeps along, ever mindful of the hazards. A mother might even look up, stop scrubbing a shirt, and wave to a passing motorist whose wheels roll inches from her tiny baby. With the influx of cars in the capital, it seems as if there should be more accidents than there are. But almost nobody gets hurt. It must be their good karma.

Although the street bustles, the activity lacks purpose in a delightful way. Surrounding the buildings, small apple orchards add agreeably to the congestion and give shade. Students in their blue gho and kira uniforms are everywhere, sitting alone or going about in groups.

On the hill above the school, where the road winds further, there are more Bhutanese houses and apartment buildings loaded with bric-a-brac gingerbread; and beyond them, at the top of the road, is the Institute for Traditional Medicine.

Down below the school, in front of the mayor's house, someone is always using the communal water spigot under the big oak tree—having a bath, washing his hair, or washing buckets of clothes. Physically, it is a messy life that belies the precision and meticulous quality of the art the people of Kawajangsa produce.

There used to be a little canteen directly across from the school, where teachers and students sat outside, enjoying the sun and playing carrom, a game like pool, in which little disks are flicked into pockets at the corners of a board about a yard square. The object is to get all your disks into the pockets, flicking a white disk with the end of your middle finger, as a cue ball is hit with a pool cue in pool, to aim and propel the colored disks. But the canteen's owner received a plot of land from the king, so he moved away a few years ago. The canteen closed and everyone moved down the street to play carrom in front of a small shop.

The village men and women have retained a strong faith, because the arts of Bhutan are part of their religion. Painting a thanka or sculpting a statue or holy object is a pious act. Still, the inhabitants of Kawajangsa are completely devoted to having a good time. And they are very good at it.

Two shops at the curve in the road across from the Painting School are the only places to buy essentials in the area. Both shops carry roughly the same things: eggs and local cheese, soft drinks, biscuits, drawing books for the students, pencils, incense, oil for butter lamps, plastic combs, hair oil, shampoo, soap, socks, rice, chili pickle, beer, tea, sugar, powdered milk, and a few other necessary items.

Many of the town's artisans live on this hillock, and their houses form a crazy patchwork. Walking up past the houses you can hear the steady *thwack, thwack* of women weaving and the sound of pressure cookers intermittently hissing as their valves release steam. Everyone cooks with pressure cookers in Bhutan. Since the stoves are fueled by propane gas in cylinders, it's economical and practical to cook fast. The steam cooks everything quickly and most of the minerals and nutrients stay in the food. Also, it makes the meat tender. The local meat is very tough. The cows aren't fed hormones to make their meat tender as in the West, and walking up and down the mountains builds strong muscles. Clanging cowbells and children's laughter add to the din.

When we worked at the Painting School, Namgay was the carrom champion of Kawajangsa. In late October, near the end of the school year, some of the teachers and students would pack the ramshackle canteen next to the school during lunch and crowd around the small board, watching the games. Namgay, sitting in a chair in front of the open window, would take on the other teachers and some of the students as well as assorted locals. Students even poked their heads in through the window to watch. Everyone tried to beat him; they never did. His hand-eye coordination was amazing. It was so much fun to watch.

Namgay's appearance and dress were immaculate; with his dazzling white *lage*—the eight-inch-wide detachable white cuffs men wore on their gho sleeves—his polished black dress shoes, and his slender frame, he looked different from the other teachers. He was one of them, but somehow apart. *Could anything happen between us?* I'd ask myself. I doubted it. We came from such different places. But still, I thought, Bhutan was a place where improbable things tended to happen.

It was a time in my life that I remember as going purely on instinct, like maneuvering a canoe through rapids. We did seem to be running into each other on the stairs at school with more frequency. The other teachers at the school told me that he liked me; he wanted to talk more with me but was shy.

I was used to their teasing, and I gave it back to them. But he seemed above their crass comments. "Don't tease him," I admonished them. They made the most ethereal, meticulous Buddhist paintings and sculptures, but they had the sensibilities of Teamsters. They were Quince, Snug, Flute, Starveling, Bottom, and Snout in *A Midsummer Night's Dream*. I adored them.

"This is no joke!" they'd respond, earnestly. I started to look at him and pay attention.

The teachers, all male, and as loud and boisterous as Namgay was reserved, continued: "Look, you are so old and you never married. Lopen Namgay is so old and he never married." They would give a sideways glance as if to say I could put it together for myself.

"Okay," I'd say, "I'll marry him. But only because you are already taken—I am so sad you have a wife. You didn't wait for me!"

"But in Bhutan you can have more than one wife!"

"No way," I'd say. "I'm not going to be second wife. Second wife has to scrub your filthy lage."

In fact, polygamy was common until only a few decades ago in the villages of Bhutan—all over the Himalayan region, in fact, so sometimes men or women would marry several partners. Occasionally a man would marry sisters or a woman would marry brothers. It was an indication of wealth, a good way to ensure that property stayed in the family and the fields stayed full of hands. In these underpopulated valleys where most people rarely left or even moved around, it was a survival tactic. These days polygamy is uncommon. Certainly none of the instructors at the school had multiple wives.

I started learning more Dzongkha so I could talk with Namgay. He understood some English, but I was sure he wouldn't speak English to me at school. He wasn't fluent. At home, I got my friend and neighbor, Chuni, to teach me words and phrases so I could say more to him.

One day at school, Namgay and I found ourselves alone in the office in between classes. I asked him in Dzongkha if he was married.

"Amsu me," he said, emphatically. "Not married."

"Do you have children?" I asked. One never knows.

"No children," he said.

His walk was graceful and his movements spare. He seemed terribly self-contained. "He is a Buddha," said Lopen Dorji.

I loved to watch him critique his students' work. They'd make elaborate pencil drawings based on the standard iconography—Buddha heads, arms and hands, lotus flowers, and mythological animals—on grids they would draw on the paper. Or they sometimes drew with a stylus on slate dusted with chalk. When paper was in short supply, this was the traditional way to learn. All of the students' drawings looked faultlessly rendered to me, but when they went to Namgay's desk at the front of the class, he would look at the drawings for a few seconds and then, with a red pen, lengthen a forearm half a millimeter or correct the angle of some deity's foot ever so slightly, minuscule adjustments that made the drawing perfect. I suppose all of the teachers had this talent and strong eye for detail, but I was only interested in watching Namgay.

Soon, we were talking every day, and the subject matter was limited to my vocabulary in Dzongkha. We talked about the weather, the school, students, and food. Although I didn't allow myself to think seriously about marriage, I suppose it was in the back of my mind.

At home, I told Chuni that there was one lopen at the school I liked.

"Who is this?" she asked. Bhutan is so small, everybody knows everybody else.

In fact, she knew his family. "They are very religious people," she said. "In their village in Trongsa there is a stream, and people say that if you drink the water from this stream you will have a beautiful singing voice. I'm sure he can sing!" she finished, triumphant. She said this like it was the lone attribute—the missing link—to make us a perfect match.

An interesting idea, but not quite the endorsement I was looking for. Still, there was a profound sense of mystery that I felt about him. I found American men much more predictable in their behavior by virtue of living in the same culture. To be living in, but really outside, the Bhutanese culture was an odd position. I liked so much about Bhutan, but there was so much I didn't understand.

To this day, there are many things that puzzle me about Namgay. But it doesn't preclude me from loving him. Part of loving is just relishing the mystery and the improbability of it all. It's a quirk of my DNA, and it makes me rely more on my intuition.

Using and honing intuition changes one's thinking. An American friend who visited Bhutan from the U.S. commented on the frenetic level of physical energy everyone seems to have in the U.S. There's all this multitasking, and we have to schedule our days and carefully plan so we get everything done. We talk more in the U.S. The opposite is true here. Multitasking is not in evidence yet, and the pace is much slower. But the mental energy here, the level of awareness that comes from paying attention, from having less stuff around and having less on our calendars, is formidable.

In the West, many have lost their sense of wonder about things. If miracles happen, how can we possibly know about them? We are too busy to notice. We've gained wonderful things such as wealth and efficiency, but I think we've lost a great deal of perception—sixth sense, insight, call it what you like. When you're occupied every minute of the day, there's simply no time for this kind of awareness.

Namgay said he would come to my house for tea, where we could enjoy each other's company away from school and where our every movement wouldn't be monitored by the other lopens or the students.

The day he came, he brought me a small Dzongkha-English dictionary. It reminded me of my grandmother, who always said there were only three things that were proper for a gentleman to give a lady as a gift: a book, a parasol, and gloves. My sister and I used to laugh at this antiquated idea. Now it was happening to me. Soon, as the visits amassed, we had a pile of dictionaries between us in my little sitting room. We taught each other English and Dzongkha. Namgay also brought me walnuts, rice, eggs, and butter. He brought me weavings by his sisters, and *ara*, a locally brewed wine that tastes a little like sake. This meant we were courting.

Instinct only goes so far. And I wasn't that evolved. I was getting increasingly agitated as the school year ended, and it was clear that Namgay liked me and I liked him. I felt like I was in junior high school again, and it wasn't a great feeling. I was getting dumber and dumber, losing an enormous number of IQ points, forgetting to turn the water off in the bathtub, forgetting to eat, smoking too many cigarettes, leaving my purse in the canteen, becoming a bundle of insecurity. Wondering all the time what he was feeling gave me pimples. I wanted to move things forward. Did he want to kiss me like I wanted to kiss him? I was so attracted to him. I saw the way he looked at me. He liked me. But he seemed so serene. And he didn't do anything. I wanted to jump into his arms every time I saw him. Was he not feeling this, too?

The day classes ended for the year, I was sitting on the front steps of the school, looking at some papers the students had written. I thought all the other teachers had left for the day. Then Namgay walked up and stood beside me. I could see his legs with long black socks and smell lavender soap, his smell. He didn't say anything. He stood there for a minute or so; and then, without looking up at him, I said, *"Nga cheu lu gaye."* I like you.

He said, *"Nga cheu lu GAYE."* I LIKE you.

I was in a state of total confusion. I got up off the step, collected my things, and walked—then ran—all the way to Chuni's house and rang her bell urgently.

When she came to the door I said, "I told him I liked him!"

"And?"

"Not good," I said. "He corrected my pronunciation!"

"What?"

"I said, '*Nga cheu lu gaye,*' and then he said, '*Nga cheu lu GAYE!*'" I was so used to having Bhutanese correct my not-very-good Dzongkha that if they repeated what I said, I just assumed that they were correcting my pronunciation.

Chuni looked at me like I was from outer space. "Idiot! He wasn't correcting your pronunciation. He was saying he liked you, too."

"How do you know?"

"Oh my God. You are really a mess."

"Do you think he likes me?"

"Yes," she said and laughed. "Relax. And come in the house. It's getting cold outside."

After that, things between Namgay and me started to happen.

It was mid-December, and we were to have a school-closing ceremony on December 17, the Bhutanese National Day. The air in Kawajangsa became thick with excitement and anticipation and the sounds of hammering: the building of welcoming gates and review stands. Exams were over and everyone was relieved. A few days before the ceremony, three large white Bhutanese tents were erected on the lawn of the school. They were room-sized rectangular pavilions made of canvas, with walls on three sides. The fourth side opened to the parade ground.

Whenever a celebration is imminent in Bhutan, up go the tents. Painted on each of these were the Eight Auspicious Symbols, or lucky signs, images one sees throughout India and the Himalayas. The signs, originally Hindu symbols, have evolved over the centuries to represent parts of the Buddha's body as well as elements of the dharma, or Buddha's teachings.

The lotus flower represents purity of body, speech, and mind and is a symbol of compassion; the endless knot symbolizes wisdom and love; the parasol protects against illness and other harmful forces; the golden fish represents freedom and emancipation from suffering; the treasure vase symbolizes long life and prosperity; the right-turning conch shell, whose sound when blown spreads the dharma, means "Wake up!"; the victory banner symbolizes the triumph of body, speech, and mind over death, ignorance, and suffering; and the dharma wheel represents the law of karma and Buddha's teachings. The beautiful white tents with the vibrant lucky signs gave the school grounds a festive air.

Various dignitaries from the government would be coming around 10 A.M. to hand out awards to the students and make speeches. The students had been working for weeks on an entertainment program that included a sports competition, a drama, songs, dance, and a comedy skit or two. Of course, there was also an exhibition of student art.

Early on the morning of the closing ceremony, some of the staff and students began to prepare a luncheon of many meat curries, rice, snacks, and tea, cooking in big pots over open fires near the kitchen. Others arranged rugs, tables, and chairs in the tents to make the guests comfortable. Some students were chopping the tall weeds in the flowerbeds, and others were sitting in groups on the lawn or practicing their parts. They were nervous and excited because during the ceremony they would find out their class rankings and whether or not they had passed to the next level.

By now, everyone in the school, even the students, was rooting for Namgay and me. In a certain segment of Bhutanese society, this was how people courted: with the help and encouragement of the community. It was like a barn dance in the Old West with the schoolmarm and her suitor. The age-old customs hadn't changed, hadn't been influenced by television, self-help gurus, the Internet, online dating, bars, or any of the things we have in the U.S. It was a courtship where almost everything was unspoken, a silent minuet. There was loads of chemistry, though. I have to say it was remarkable and gripping, the most interesting thing I've ever done.

I kept asking myself, *What are you doing?* But some force would say don't doubt. Never doubt. And so I didn't. But I was clearly in unmapped territory. In the U.S., people dated. They went to movies or dinners or football games or parties. There was a lot of conversation, even when there wasn't much chemistry or attraction. It's as if, in the U.S., we talked in order to simulate chemistry. But it was the opposite for Namgay and me. We didn't seem to need it.

I didn't have much to do, so I walked around to see if I could help out, and I also did what I had done for the last few months, which was to try to casually run into

Namgay. He was easy to spot because he was all over the place. He was adept at the finer points of *driglam namzha,* Bhutanese etiquette, so he was in charge of arranging the ceremony. He barked orders to students, who rushed here or there to complete tasks or fetch things. At one point, he was busy at the flagpole folding a Bhutanese flag so that at the start of the day's festivities, when he raised it, the flag would unfurl and shower bright yellow and orange marigold petals. I stayed out of his way.

After a short time, I saw him with a couple of students, standing in front of one of the tents. One of the girls had a camera and was going to take a picture. He saw me and raised his hand, motioning for me to come and be in the picture. My world turned. This was a new thing; he rarely acknowledged or spoke to me when students were around.

Soon the dignitaries and guests arrived and everyone was in position for the opening ceremony. After the national anthem, Namgay unfurled the flag. On cue, petals rained down. The air was thick with the smell of juniper incense. There was a solemn prayer, an offering to deities, and an homage to the chief guest, then the sports competition got under way. The principal had planned a long jump, a high jump, and other tests of athletic skills. Just before the long jump started, I was standing on the lawn and talking with a group of girls. I heard the principal announce in a jolly voice that *all* of the faculty were required to participate in the long jump. Everyone laughed, delighted. I could have begged off, but Namgay might think I was a bad sport.

Next to the school building, there was an area sectioned off by sticks and strings to make the long-jump runway, and at its end was a pit with sand. It looked ominous, if not a little dangerous. Remember, I was wearing a floor-length kira. I also had on high heels, the most important accessory for fashion-forward kira-wearers. Two students, one on either side of the pit, were there to mark the jump with a tape measure. As I watched, dreading my turn, a couple of the more eager teachers took their turns, flailing their arms and legs for effect, landing on various parts of their anatomy. The crowd howled with delight.

There couldn't be a more restricting garment to run in than a kira, much less make a long, graceful jump. But I didn't want to stick out or appear not to play well with others. I was the foreigner. So I had to try harder. This seemed to take precedence over my physical safety. When the principal called my name, I felt real fear. I was afraid of falling and injuring myself. But I knew it was best not to waste time: the longer I procrastinated, the larger audience I would draw. The crowd of students, teachers, and assorted guests, their appetite already whetted by the performances of the other teachers, were anxious for more spectacle. And what better spectacle than the American English teacher, Miss Linda, who could always be counted on to do something just a little different? It was a setup, and I was a willing participant. The students laughed and cheered and cajoled me. "Do it, Miss!"

All eyes, including Namgay's, were on me. Everyone cheered as I made my way to the long jump. I kicked off my high heels, hiked up my kira, positioned myself at the head of the run, and prayed. Then I made a running start and, at the edge of the pit, leapt out into the air. It wasn't such a long jump, but I landed in the cool sand, miraculously crouching on my feet. I put my arms out in front of me to steady myself as I pulled myself erect like an Olympic gymnast, a nice touch that surprised even me. The crowd roared its approval. "Good job!" one of my students called out, mimicking my classroom voice.

Mine wasn't anywhere near the winning jump, or the second, or the third. I came in fourth, actually, and best of all, I didn't fall on my face or crack my ankle. I didn't dare look at Namgay. I felt like every part of me had taken a great leap of faith—a great, long running jump—a commitment to a lifetime in Bhutan, to a marriage, to love.

I could hardly eat any of the enormous lunch that was served, buffet style in one of the tents. The students ate in groups on the lawn and the dignitaries were served in comfortable chairs in another tent. After lunch, we all assembled on the lawn in front of the dais to watch the students receive their awards. I was standing near the back of the large crowd of students, teachers, and friends, a crowd of about 100 people. There were even some tourists on the fringes of the lawn who had disembarked from a large bus, an audience to the audience. Then people began to whisper, "Miss! Miss! Miss!"

I was Miss. They were summoning me, directing me, indicating with their arms that I should move to the front of the group. The crowd parted Red Sea–like as students and teachers, looking at me, squeezed together to make a clear path so that I could move up. Then I saw Namgay standing at the front of the crowd. He was smiling, his hand and arm outstretched, a space beside him cleared. Here was this sweet, shy man summoning me into his world, publicly recognizing me, asking me to stand with him in front of the students and teachers and guests—in front of the whole world—well, at least the world of Kawajangsa, the only world that mattered.

Slowly, I walked up the aisle and took my place beside him. I looked at him. He smiled. He took my hand! It was a sweet, wonderful moment, one of the best moments of my life. Even now, years later, I remember that feeling of intensity, the feeling of the whole cosmos coming together in a defining instant. Life was huge and wonderful. I felt ten feet tall.

I don't remember who graduated, who was first in each of the eight classes, or anything else about the ceremony. I was just aware of Namgay standing beside me, the feeling of his hand, and this amazing thing that he had done to move things forward and seal our fate—his own rather remarkable leap.

If you're going through hell, keep going.

— WINSTON CHURCHILL

To Love and
to Cherish

It was winter break from school when Namgay
and I started thinking of marriage. We continued the
Dzongkha and English lessons, and there were lots of
sidelong looks and grazing of hands as we both reached
for the same book. It was really Victorian, intriguing,
wonderful, heart-racing stuff. I wasn't sure what might
ultimately happen, but my life had taken a turn since
I'd moved to Bhutan. I was used to being in unexplored
territory. Namgay was not only a teacher but also a great
cook, and he could chop wood and lift three times his
weight. He could sew, plant a garden, and herd animals.
He could rewire a house and repair a broken lock. He was
dependable, protective, polished, handsome, hardworking, and religious. He was highly evolved spiritually. He
could perform a variety of rituals to appease numerous
deities. While not the attributes I was accustomed to in
American men, all these things matter a great deal in
Bhutan. Namgay was a catch.

His education had been quite different from mine. He liked to draw. When he was a child, he lived with his Uncle Lama, and paper and pencils were hard to come by so he drew in the dirt with a stick. Because Namgay exhibited some early promise as an artist, instead of becoming a monk he was sent to the National Art School in Thimphu to study thanka painting. After 8 years at the school and a 15-year apprenticeship painting temples all over Bhutan, he went to work at the school, teaching students to paint thankas.

Since much of Bhutanese society is matrilineal, the man usually moves in with the woman and her family when they marry. In the villages, some marriages might be arranged, but mostly they are love matches. A marriage is often simply an agreement, but there can be a wedding puja or a celebration if the couple has a little money.

When we decided to marry, I said I wanted to move to Namgay's house. I had no property or family; my house was rented. He thought it was a bad idea, that it would be too difficult, since my house had a large water heater, among other amenities, and his house had no hot water.

I believed that since I was in Bhutan, marrying a Bhutanese, I should make an effort to live like a Bhutanese. I was already used to adapting to their way of life—or so I thought. And I knew if we lived on the other side of town in my little cottage, Namgay's family would feel awkward and might not readily visit us. Anyway, I reasoned, if it didn't work out we could always move. I suppose I was lulled into a false sense of security. The truth is, all Bhutanese go out of their way to be kind to foreigners. It's just part of who they are. So what it boiled down to was that for about two and a half years, the time I spent living in Bhutan before I married Namgay, the whole country had basically been babysitting me. Once, years before, when I was moving from my rented house in Semtokha to the cottage I lived in when I met Namgay, I hired a taxi to move me and my stuff, which was several suitcases, numerous baskets of books, and a few pots and pans. The taxi driver was kind; he made several trips back and forth carting my things, and he even helped me move the stuff out of my old house into the new one. My only sadness was that, somewhere between the two houses, I lost one of my shoes.

A month went by; and one day as I came out of a shop, clutching shopping bags filled with rice and vegetables, someone shouted, "Oh, Cinderella! Miss Cinderella!" It was the taxi driver who had helped me move, grinning big, driving slowly down the street, steering the taxi with one hand and waving my missing shoe out the window with the other.

Namgay eventually agreed to let me give up the cottage and join him in his apartment in his sister's house.

We spent weeks talking in broken English and Dzongkha with dictionaries spread before us and a fire blazing in the stove, learning each other's language and deciding our future. He said I had to stop smoking because it hurt Guru Rinpoche's eyes. And every time I lit a cigarette, according to Namgay, a *Dakini*, a female manifestation of enlightened energy in Vajrayana Buddhism, fell from the sky. Addiction aside, I couldn't be responsible for that; so, with great effort, I quit.

After several weeks, Namgay invited me to his house to meet his family.

The day I was supposed to go, a wave of anxiety hit me, and my knees actually started to wobble. In my life I have hardly ever had wobbly knees. I'm not a wobbly-knee kind of person. But this was bigger than anything I had ever done—a giant leap into a life so radically different that I could hardly imagine it. I knew I was intruding in an enormous way on Namgay's family's life. Once I visited them, I felt there would be no turning back. It would mean that for all practical purposes we were married, since this is how village people in Bhutan view marriage.

Of course it was a huge gamble for me, but I still marvel at the chance they took. They were, and are, a very traditional Buddhist family. Namgay, his two sisters, and their families all lived near each other in Kawajangsa and took care of their mother, who split her time equally between her daughters' households. The eldest sister, Choki, was married to a wood-carver named Dhendup. Karma, the second sister, had a husband, Pema, who was a thanka painter who taught at the National Art School with Namgay and me.

They could have been voted Bhutanese family least likely to have anything to do with a foreigner; and they were some of the shyest, most unassuming people I have ever met. They were not well-to-do; they were polite, hardworking, and religious. They lived their faith and never missed an opportunity to be kind. It's not that they had anything against foreigners. It's just that they would never have had a chance to meet one, since so few foreigners live in Bhutan. I might as well have been from outer space. But they were about to have me full force among them. This is what made my knees shake. Buddhists say: if you can't help, at least don't hurt. I so didn't want to hurt. And knowing that we were from such dissimilar universes made me worry that we wouldn't be able to meet somewhere in the middle. I felt like an invader.

That Saturday morning in January, the sun was bright and the birds danced and screeched in the garden as I dressed myself in a nice kira. Then I changed it and put on another, then another, until all of the kiras I owned were strewn about the house. Nothing looked right or felt right, and my house looked like it had been looted. I fled to my neighbor Chuni's house, and she said I looked fine in what I was wearing. "Don't worry," she said. "They're nice people."

"That's what I'm worried about," I said. Namgay and I had decided to make it work. They didn't have a choice. Whatever happened, they had to come along for the ride.

I'd bought an enormous tin of Danish butter cookies and a big sack of walnuts to give to Namgay's mother. I walked down to the road and got a taxi.

When I walked up the stairs to the front door, Namgay's nephew came to greet me. It turned out that Namgay wasn't home. He had gone to the vegetable market to shop for the week's produce. His nephew, who looked to be in high school, said that Namgay would be right back. I heard myself say in a whisper, "Oh, well, okay, I'll come back . . ." I turned to leave.

"Wait," he called. "Come in and have a cup of tea."

I drank sitting cross-legged on a pillow on the floor in Namgay's temple room. Most houses in Bhutan have a temple room, or *choshom,* which means "altar." They might not have indoor plumbing, but there is usually a room with an elaborately carved and brightly painted wooden altar covering one wall. On the glass-enclosed shelves of the altar are the gilded statues of household

deities. Families in Bhutan, depending on their pro-
clivities, almost always have images of Guru Rinpoche,
or his wrathful manifestation Dorji Drolo; Shabdrung
Ngawang Namgyal; Chana Dorji, a powerful protector;
Chenrezig, the manifestation of compassion; or one of
the Taras—White Tara for long-term wishes and desires
and good marriage and good health, or Green Tara for
more short-term needs like money and safe journeys.

The people of Bhutan put much of their wealth into
these rooms. If the family has a little money, the statues
are big, elaborate, and numerous; and there are thankas,
framed in silk, hanging on the walls. In front of the statues on the altar, there is a symbolic offering of seven bowls
of water. Offerings to the deities shouldn't be a measure
of wealth, and water is a leveler: anyone can offer it, so it
is offered every morning. I noticed in Namgay's temple
room there were no thankas, only posters of deities and
pictures of thankas. Although Namgay paints some of the
most beautiful thankas I have ever seen, he keeps none of
them. They are all for other people.

There were red and blue flowers on the altar in a great
jumble of antique brass and silver vases, and the smell of
sandalwood incense wafted across the room. It mingled
with the smell of dust and the mildew of the ancient
prayer books, wrapped in yellow silk in a glass case in the
corner. Great, intricate butter sculptures, called *torma*, in
rows behind the water bowls added to the overwrought
appearance of the shrine. White obelisks with red, blue,
green, and yellow flowers on the tops reflected light
from several rows of butter lamps—oil in silver chalices
with cotton wicks—that give off perceptible heat along
with light. The butter lamps, so called because in olden
times they were actually fueled by butter, were full of

melted vegetable oil; and everything, especially the golden statues, glistened in the candlelight. A red silk canopy rimmed in yellow silk covered most of the ceiling, making the room tentlike and cozy, and everything had a sepia tint from years of candle smoke. There were so many bits of silk, wooden crosses with pieces of string threaded through them to form diamond shapes, things that might catch on fire—but never did. It was a beautiful external expression of the family's faith.

In the corner, against the wall, there was a canvas sewn to a wooden frame—a thanka that someone, perhaps the nephew, had left off painting. There were small bowls of bright paint and some brushes on the floor around it. The thanka was a little forest scene with an elephant, a monkey, a rabbit, and a bird standing next to a beautiful tree. The monkey was sitting on the elephant's back, the rabbit was on the monkey's back, and the bird, who sat on the monkey's head, was reaching for one of the tree's bright red berries. You see this image all over Bhutan, painted on the walls of houses and temples; it illustrates the parable of the Four Faithful Friends, who embody the spirit of cooperation and friendship. The friends help each other and ensure their own survival. Namgay's nephew, named Dorji, was in class 11, and he said Namgay was teaching him to paint thankas during the school holiday.

Once, out of the corner of my eye, I thought I saw an old woman dart past the open temple-room door. It must have been Namgay's mother, Lhamo. If I had been new to Bhutan, I would have thought this odd—that she was trying to avoid me. But I knew it was because she was just too bashful to have me see her. Already the family was jittery. Namgay's American friend had come.

I remembered what my neighbor Chuni had said to me once: sometimes she hears a voice or just has a feeling in her body that tells her she needs to stay put and not move. "When in doubt, do nothing." It's a fundamental of Daoism, *wu wei*, the innate knowledge of when to act and when not to act, sometimes described as "acting without acting." That made enormous sense to me. So I burrowed in and absorbed the calming ambiance of the beautiful temple room.

Then from the window, I saw Namgay walking up the street. He was wearing a beautiful woven gho and carrying a recycled rice sack full of vegetables in one hand and a cardboard tray of eggs tied with string in the other. I heard his footsteps on the stairs, and my heart pounded. There was a flutter of voices in the hallway as his relatives told him in hushed, urgent tones that I was in the temple room. I heard Namgay giving orders in Dzongkha. He was making arrangements to feed me, as I was an honored guest.

He came in and greeted me with exaggerated enthusiasm. "HellOOOOO!" he said like Steve Martin's wild and crazy guy—without the irony. An American woman had never come to see him and his family, but he was trying to make it seem like it happened every day. His awkwardness made me ache. The friendly, relaxed feeling we'd had on those long visits to my house was gone. I was in his territory now. We would need time to adjust.

Our conversation was stilted; then he disappeared. He came back after a few minutes with another cup of tea and some biscuits and once again evaporated. To Americans this is very strange behavior, but any Bhutanese would do the same thing. Bhutanese must give the visitor the best, most comfortable place in the house to sit, and then they must feed the guest the best food they have. Conversation is optional—food is not. Namgay and his family were in his kitchen cooking me a big lunch, as would any respectable Bhutanese family. So I waited alone, as was the custom.

With Namgay home, my nervousness gave way to a sense of adventure, if not quite optimism. Now I was enjoying this visit tremendously. There was a nice breeze blowing through the open window. The house was on a hill just above the Painting School. The view from the window was Thimphu proper surrounded by green mountains and, above them, clouds. It was a scene of stunning beauty. It felt like the right place to be.

After an hour or so, Namgay appeared again with an enormous bowl of red rice and some *phak sha pha,* or dried, aged pork fat, considered a delicacy in Bhutan. He sat the food in front of me on the floor, smiled, and then left the room again. I waited for several minutes to see if he would return with food for himself. It is typical for guests to eat alone in a traditional Bhutanese household, but Namgay and I, when he came to my house, ate together American-style. He didn't come back.

I stood up, smoothed my kira, picked up the bowls of rice and pork, and walked into Namgay's kitchen. There they all were: Namgay, his mother, and his nephew, sitting on cow hides on the kitchen floor enjoying their meal. I stood in the doorway. They jumped up, looking alarmed as if something terrible had happened, or as if they had been caught doing something illegal. Namgay rushed over to take the bowls of food from my hands.

I laughed and said in Dzongkha, "Please sit down. I want to eat with you. I'm lonely in the temple room!"

Everyone looked at me, surprised. This was highly

irregular. Then they laughed, too. "*Toup!*" Namgay said. "Okay!"

He set my bowls of food on the floor between his and his mother's. I sat down on a bearskin rug between them, and we all had a nice meal together. Our first of many.

It was getting late, and Namgay's mother said I should sleep in the temple room. I hadn't planned to spend the night. I hadn't planned anything, really.

They made me a comfortable bed from rugs and blankets, and I took off my belt and *koma,* the two gold and silver brooches that fasten the kira at the shoulder, and crawled into the little nest. Almost everybody in Bhutan sleeps this way—no mattress, just whatever is available to put on the floor and cover up with. In the mornings, the bedding is stored away or hung on clotheslines to air out. When I talk with visitors to Bhutan, the universal complaint is the uncomfortable mattresses in the hotels. If only they knew the hotel mattresses were actually the best Bhutan has to offer.

As the family slept, I lay awake in the dark, too excited and amazed to even close my eyes. It was true. I was marrying Namgay. All of us, Namgay, his family, and I, were starting a life together. What would it be like? I had no idea. The unknowable quality of what was about to happen didn't make me feel anxious. I felt wonderful, as if a big, grand adventure was about to unfold. All I had to do was show up. I was in some kind of suspended state of euphoria—the place you go just before something really monumental happens. I felt invincible, because I knew that whatever did happen, I was in a wonderful place with these lovely, remarkable people.

Once, years later, Namgay asked me why I loved him and I said because he had a good heart, he was handsome, and his work was close to God. Lying in the temple room, I realized that now, because I was marrying Namgay, I would also be married to Bhutan. When you marry a foreigner, you also marry the country. I had never been so happy.

We had several weddings. The first was traditional Buddhist, because it's important to appease the deities. A *sip*, or Bhutanese astrologer, chose March 10, 2000, saying it was auspicious. It was a glorious, cloudless day, as most March days are in Bhutan, with a cool, crisp wind as a reminder of winter. We were glad for the chill in the air after several hours in the small temple room with hundreds of butter lamps generating substantial heat. Five red-robed monks and one lama crowded into the temple room with Namgay and me. They blew eight-foot horns, beat ceremonial drums, and chanted prayers for our well-being and happiness. Namgay looked handsome in a red-and-yellow silk gho that had been woven by his sister Karma many years before in anticipation of his marriage; I had an elaborate woven silk wedding kira, as is the custom, made of many different shades of red and pink. Only his family and a few of our friends— maybe 40 people—attended. They came into the temple room one by one and presented us with katas.

Since my family couldn't come, a Bhutanese friend stood in and performed their duties. All day and into the evening, Namgay and I sat together on pillows in the temple room of his family's house. After the ceremony there was food and drink, followed by dancing.

I moved to his house with two suitcases of clothes, a car, a refrigerator, a few dishes and pots, a small CD player and some CDs, and a new mattress—my worldly possessions. There are no dowries in Buddhist Bhutan.

Since I was a foreigner, the Royal Government required that we have a civil ceremony in the province where the groom was born. So, a couple of months later, we made the six-hour drive to Trongsa Dzong. We arrived the night before and stayed at a little inn in the small town of Trongsa.

At the morning ceremony in the judge's chamber, I wore a kira and a *rachu,* an embroidered ceremonial scarf, traditionally long and red, worn over the left shoulder, that women have to wear when they enter a government building. Namgay wore a gho and a *kabney,* a shawl-like scarf of raw silk that is draped around the body and then over one shoulder. All Bhutanese men must wear them in the dzongs. The judge, sitting behind his large desk, performed the ritual, reading out the equivalent of a civil ceremony as we stood before him. I had no idea what he was saying, but Namgay prompted me to say the Dzongkha equivalent of "I do."

It was a solemn affair until the end. The thrimpon, or judge, said that if either one of us had a problem with the other, we must report back to him immediately. We laughed and left his office for his assistant's office next door, where we sat in front of his big, messy desk and signed endless, enormous ledgers that attendants kept producing, a remnant of the old British-Indian system, where everything we signed had to be accompanied by beautiful, elaborate stamps. Of course, an office peon appeared with a big tray of tea. A large group of villagers, in the dzong to visit the court or conduct government business, stood outside the office, peeking in. In Trongsa, a foreign woman marrying a Bhutanese man was unusual, if not unprecedented.

We had to produce witnesses to cosign our marriage certificate. My witness, or my "bridesmaid," was the lovely Tibetan woman Aum Rinzy, who owned the hotel in Trongsa. As a tourist, over the years, I had stayed at her place many times and eaten in her wonderful kitchen with the big window from which I could see almost the whole of Trongsa valley, narrow and snaking and covered in virgin forest. She was delighted and amused that I was marrying a man from her village. She had four husbands of her own, all brothers.

We were having a lunch at her hotel afterward, so as soon as she gave the marriage certificate her thumbprint signature, she hurried back to organize the cooking. The simple, quick lunch we had ordered became elaborate and very festive, as it stretched into the evening with impromptu music and dance and, of course, ara. Nearly the whole town showed up at her little inn to wish us, the American woman and the "local boy," *tashi delek*—good luck.

It was moving to celebrate our wedding in Trongsa, and to know I'd married into an old, religious, very traditional family whose ancestral home was Chendebji, a well-known village in Trongsa District, about 25 miles west. The village sits on the side of a big hill, on the edge of the Black Mountains, which are as daunting and mysterious-looking as their name implies. Chendebji means "the place where a big cypress tree grows," but now the legendary tree is gone. That's too bad, because according to ancient texts, eight people could sleep in the hollows made between its trunk and its massive roots.

In ancient times, the people of Chendebji were gatekeepers, responsible for controlling traffic from both eastern and western Bhutan to the palace of Kuenga

Rabten on the other side of the district, and so the covered Maleyzam Bridge below the village would be removed during periods of conflict, especially during the time of the second king, Jigme Wangchuck, or if the king was indisposed and didn't want visitors.

Since many people would come to call on the king, the village *chipon,* a position that was rotated among the households of Chendebji, would be responsible for either allowing prospective visitors to pass or turning them away, depending upon the pleasure of the king. The visitors would usually be compelled to give a little endowment to the chipon, so the people of the village must have been well off.

A local deity named Gyelp Dungley Karpo safeguards Chendebji. At one time, the village was large, with over 100 households, but now there are only 22. Every household has a name and a ranking, decreed by the king, and Namgay's family household name was *Togto.* Its ranking was number two. The family had status in the village, because nine lamas have come, consecutively, from the household; and each of them has served as the Lama of Wangdue Goempa, a large temple and monk school in Wangdue Phodrang. Namgay's ancestral home seemed like it was out of Middle Earth. The only things missing were hobbits.

Besides his immediate family, Namgay has many aunts, uncles, and cousins. His father, now deceased, was an astrologer. After we married, Namgay told me that his father had prophesied our marriage. I would come from very far away, from a place that no one knew. He told Namgay to wait for me. He said we had been together before, married in the 17th century, at the confluence of the Mo Chu and the Po Chu, the mother and father rivers, in Punakha. When I first heard the story, I admit I viewed it with some skepticism. Now, I am skeptical about almost nothing. That's what comes from living an unconventional life.

I don't know how we got through the first six months of marriage. For me it was like India, a place I find simultaneously wonderful and horrible, and I'm sure Namgay felt the same. No amount of laying groundwork or talking prepared either of us. I remember the time in a vague, detached way, like scenes from an odd, but fantastic movie. It felt as though it was happening to someone else.

Namgay says now that he felt like he was living with a stranger. Evidently, he found my behavior somewhat erratic. Okay, I was a little bit moody, and I came completely unglued one night when he chased a rat with a broom. I heard him banging around in the kitchen for several minutes, got out of bed, and went in just in time to see a rat the size of a Chihuahua hop onto the sill and leap out the open window into the black night. I cried for hours and couldn't seem to stop, even with lavish amounts of consoling by Namgay. The next morning, our sweet neighbors sent over food, and I felt ashamed. They must have heard me crying.

We were poles apart on so many things, so we gradually had to come together. We had to change or adapt almost everything we did. Instead of flushing the toilet, I had to learn to pour a bucket of water into it. Instead of a solipsistic existence living alone, I lived with Namgay, and we lived in a house that was surrounded by many neighbors. Everyone knew our business, and everyone seemed interested in my every movement. No foreigners lived in Kawajangsa, so, walking down the street, I drew stares. Little children ran after me, so I had to get used to traveling with an entourage. We welcomed visits to our house by Namgay's extended family. Namgay was much loved, and of course they wanted to meet me. I wanted them to think I was worthy of him.

Having lived my entire adult life alone, I have to say, I had developed some pretty revolting eating habits. My general philosophy of meals was: if it's messy, eat it over the sink. In fact, messy or not, there's really nothing you can't eat while standing in the kitchen. Namgay was appalled. He carefully cleaned and prepared the food, cooked it slowly, then sat and ate in the kitchen. He relished each meal and enjoyed the process. He easily spent four hours each day preparing, eating, and cleaning up from meals. Eating out of cooking pots is very bad form in Bhutan.

I was too impatient to enjoy cooking and food. When I did prepare a meal, it was hastily put together. I had never really gotten the hang of cooking in Bhutan. Everything had to be started from scratch.

Alone, I ate crackers, lovely cheese from Bumthang valley, fruits, cookies, and tea, with the occasional carrot thrown in if I could manage to peel it. If I wanted a nice, hearty meal, I went to a restaurant. He, on the other hand, needed to expand his repertoire. His diet could be summed up in one word: rice. Every meal, whether it was breakfast, lunch, or dinner, was begun by washing several cups full of rice in clean, cold water and putting them in the rice cooker. Rice is the staple food of Bhutan, as it is throughout Asia. I never cooked rice. I didn't even know how.

I liked it, and I ate it in restaurants and in other

people's houses, but the eating of rice is relentless in a Bhutanese home. Even with the limited selection of food in the markets of Thimphu, I was accustomed to more variety in my meals. After a month or so of rice for breakfast, lunch, and dinner and puffed rice for snacks with tea, I'd look at a bowl of rice and imagine myself screaming a primordial scream, hurling it through an open window, then grabbing my head and running away. But I kept my feelings in and tried to introduce pasta. It was too early in the marriage to have a full-on nervous breakdown.

Along with rice, hot chilies are the preferred food of the Bhutanese. In fact, if you took all their other food away and just gave them rice and chilies, they'd be perfectly happy. Even as young children, they learn to love hot food, and babies get the taste of hot chilies taking their mother's breast milk. Chilies are the national addiction. If I never again in my life eat chilies, I will be perfectly happy.

There is usually a curry or two to go with the rice the Bhutanese eat with every meal. The word *curry* means anything you put on rice. *Ema datse,* which is chilies cooked in melted cheese, is the national dish of Bhutan. Bhutanese are also fond of meat, and dried meat—either yak, pork fat, or beef—is popular.

I learned to cut and clean vegetables and cook them in one of our three somewhat temperamental pressure cookers. Namgay used to call them the baby, mother, and father cookers. The midsized mother cooker had a rubber gasket on its lid that wouldn't stay put. The larger father had a piece of its handle missing. But the baby was nearly perfect. I did learn to cook rice using an electric rice cooker, first washing the rice three times in cold water and stirring it around with my hand, looking for odd bits of stone and chaff, before turning the cooker on. Most important, I learned to wash my hands after I cut chilies. You only have to chop chilies and then rub your eyes once to understand that.

The minutiae of daily life, growing accustomed to each other and adapting our ways to the ways of the other, were formidable. I can remember sweeping the sitting room one day after school. Namgay just stood in the doorway watching me with a shocked look on his face.

"What is it?"

"Is that the way you sweep?"

"Apparently. What's wrong?" I asked, defensively.

Then he showed me. He took the broom and swept the room while I looked on. I saw immediately the difference between my sweeping and his sweeping. It was stunning. I was scrambled egg; he was eggs Benedict. It was the difference between someone who had swept only occasionally and someone who had swept many times a day, every day of his life—who knew the business end of a broom. He angled the broom deftly and corralled all the little dust particles with real panache. He was the Fred Astaire of sweeping.

Living several years alone in Bhutan without a washing machine, I'd perfected a "soaking method" for washing clothes. I was thinking of patenting it. I would separate the lights from the darks and put them each in a bucket of soapy water for a day or two. I'd swish them around in the water a bit, rinse, and then hang them to dry. Voilà! Namgay was appalled. He rubbed each piece of clothing vigorously with a bar of pink laundry soap and then, when it was completely infused with soap, scrubbed it with a brush—first one side and then the other—on the concrete floor of the bathroom. I found this too labor-intensive. Also, try doing it to a cashmere sweater or silk scarf. He thought I didn't get the clothes clean enough; I thought he was unnecessarily abusive to our garments. A couple of years into the marriage, we got an impartial, disinterested washing machine; and I believe this is the reason we are still married.

Those early months I remember like snapshots, such as the time I pulled a pair of black tights out of my cupboard to wear one morning. The tights, I knew, had a hole in them. But when I put them on, I saw, to my utter amazement, that Namgay had mended it. I was stunned: had I married a man who mended tights? Evidently. I tried to imagine other men I knew mending tights. I couldn't. He had been raised in a culture where many men learned to embroider and sew. I found that wonderful. Besides the level of caring and skill, the attention to detail amazed me. And it made me sad that in the U.S. we don't mend things anymore. Mending and fixing broken things is deeply satisfying.

More than a decade has passed since Namgay and I married. I believe our marriage is a testament to tolerance; it is a measure of just how much people can change. Old dogs can learn new tricks.

People were moving to the town every day from the villages. Although water is abundant in Bhutan, the city's waterworks couldn't keep up with the demand. The waterworks often conserved water by simply turning it off for a while. So parts of the town, like the crowded suburb of Kawajangsa where we lived, often had water shortages.

When I moved to Namgay's house, I asked him if

they had a water problem. By that I meant, was there a water shortage?

He said, "No. No water problem." Silly me. Looking back, I realize it was a question of semantics, as are so many things. A water problem to him would be no water in the house—and no possibility of water in the house. A dry well. Period. End of story. Access to water three days out of seven was no problem. For me, a water problem meant there wasn't water 24 hours a day, seven days a week.

But by the time I figured all of this out, I was firmly ensconced in his house in Kawajangsa, about five minutes' walk from the Painting School, where we both continued to work. I had already given up my little bungalow on the other side of town with the enormous water heater and the abundant water supply.

Otherwise, we lived in a nice apartment. There were eight small rooms: kitchen, temple room, sitting room, storeroom, toilet, and three bedrooms. In the traditional Bhutanese style, the house was whitewashed adobe, solidly built of mud, which is an excellent insulator, with wood-plank floors and windows with shutters but no glass. Our furnishings were little benches covered with Tibetan rugs and large painted chests; the bedroom had a mattress and two cupboards. I loved the spareness. The lack of clutter in the small rooms, and then the explosion of clutter in the over-the-top temple room, pleased me no end. The kitchen and bathroom were rudimentary and functional, and the house was spotlessly clean.

Like water, electricity was a challenge. There was enough power to run the rice cooker, a small space heater, and the fluorescent bulb on the ceiling of each room. But if I wanted to blow-dry my hair, I'd have to turn everything else off. Again, for Namgay this constituted no electrical problem. We just had different expectations.

Although I had lived in Bhutan for several years, I had never fully understood how ecologically and frugally most Bhutanese live. One evening after a difficult day, at the end of a long week at school, I walked up the dusty road just as the sun was going down below the mountains. I wanted desperately to take a bath. Usually we filled buckets with water, used a heating element to warm it, and washed in the bathroom, standing over the buckets. We used small plastic pitchers to scoop up water and rinse with it. Tonight, though, I wanted a real bath, and I had been thinking of it all day.

As soon as I arrived home, I got a towel, a change of clothing, and shampoo, and then turned on the bathroom tap. Nothing came out. I ran to the kitchen. We had a ten-gallon plastic bucket in the corner of the kitchen that we kept filled with water for just such situations. The bucket was empty, and there was no water coming from the kitchen tap either.

At that point, I sat down on the kitchen floor and started to cry. I cried because I was dirty and I wanted to take a bath after a hard day; I cried because I was exhausted and I felt like I wasn't tough enough; and I cried because I dearly loved Namgay and couldn't imagine living without him, but I was worried we wouldn't make it—we wouldn't beat the odds, the difficulties and stresses of an intercultural marriage, the language issues, the lack of water, all of which were stacking against us. I had come such a long way in my life. But I needed to go so much further. I had enjoyed so much privilege and comfort. I had never lived with so little luxury—or so much scarcity and change.

By the time Namgay came home about 30 minutes later, it was dark. I was still sitting on the kitchen floor, crying, with the lights off. He turned on the lights and saw me, and then he turned around and left without saying a word. He abandoned me.

That made me cry even more, until I heard his heavy footsteps on the stairs outside and the sloshing of water. He had come back lugging two enormous buckets of water from the tap in a neighbor's yard down the hill. As the water heated, he made me a cup of tea. Then he picked me up off the floor where I was still sniveling in a heap, carried me in his arms to the bathroom, undressed me, and gave me a gentle bath, like I was a temperamental but treasured child.

Then he took a bath, and by the time we had dinner and got in bed, we were happy, laughing, and very clean.

*There are, in the heart of the vast Himalayas,
some strange marketplaces where one can barter
the whirlwind of life for infinite wisdom.*

— **JETSUN MILAREPA,** *TIBETAN YOGI AND POET*

To Have and
to Hold

Traveling a little in India and Nepal had been the extent of Namgay's forays outside of Bhutan. What he knew of American culture he knew from me. We focused on the daily things we had in common, and sometimes we talked about how we were brought up. He was amazed by American affluence and liked our straightforward way of talking. Namgay thinks all Americans are remarkable, admirable people. Most of the ones he's met are educated, and he prizes education. Also, Namgay does happen to know some remarkable, admirable Americans (ahem).

I am Western educated, which gives me a certain status in Bhutan. But the status is misleading, as my education has in no way prepared me to live in this culture, and I am forever falling short of Bhutanese expectations. For example, I don't know how to program a DVD player.

"But you have such a fine education," Namgay says, exasperated and surprised.

In his eyes, my expensive and extensive Western education should afford me more aptitude.

"Yes, but with my M.F.A. degree and $6 I can buy coffee at Starbucks," I offer.

"Huh?" he says.

"Never mind. Where are the instructions?"

When we married, we decided that toward the end of the first year we'd go to the U.S. I wanted to introduce Namgay and my family to each other. And of course I wanted to show Namgay my country. Besides, I hadn't left Bhutan in over three years, so it was time I reacquainted myself with my ancestral home.

So nine months into our marriage we were on a plane headed to Bangkok. I thought that would be a good place to hang for a few days, a sort of decompression chamber before we headed to the U.S. It's still Asian, but a world-class city. Even so, there was really no way I could prepare him.

The first evening in Bangkok, I came out of the shower, and I noticed Namgay wasn't in the hotel room. I dressed quickly and looked in the hallway, the lobby, the bar. I went out on the street. He was gone. My heart racing, I ran back up to the room. He was coming back in from the balcony. He'd been watching a steady stream of airplanes as they followed flight paths to land at the airport. Throughout our stay, he spent hours watching the planes. I watched with him sometimes, and it was quite remarkable: a plane appeared every four seconds like a bright bead floating diagonally on an invisible string in the sky, then vanished amid the bright lights of Bangkok.

He grew up in a place where you couldn't see anything but birds flying in the sky. No wonder he was amazed. The airplanes in Bangkok were the first of many things I saw through Namgay's eyes, things I'd seen all my life, only now forever changed.

I was hoping Namgay would like Nashville. There are a few parallels between Tennessee, where I grew up, and Bhutan. Both places are rural, religious, and traditional, made up of mountain communities. People don't, in the case of Bhutan, and didn't, in the case of Nashville, travel so much. They stay put, so everyone tends to be only a few degrees of separation apart. Bhutan has devout Buddhists; Tennessee has devout Baptists. Manners are as important in Tennessee as they are in Bhutan. In Nashville we were raised to say, "No, ma'am" and "Yes, sir," and compared to the rest of the country, Tennesseans have good manners and a quiet grace. The Bhutanese substitute "Yes, madam," for "ma'am."

In rural Tennessee and, in fact, all over the countryside, people still look out for each other. There's a lot of social capital in both places, and both are known for their strong women: Tennessee has Steel Magnolias and Bhutan has Dragon Ladies.

Bhutanese people's exotic looks and quiet manners belie the fact that deep down they're just a bunch of good ol' boys and girls. I once took a trip to a remote part of Eastern Bhutan. Our driver, a wiry former monk who could fix anything, asked if he could put his own tape in our Land Cruiser's cassette player. In that part of the world, you never know what mysteries can come out of lax copyright laws and Asian ingenuity. "Sure," I said, and braced myself for some strange hybrid song—a Thai all-girl band covering Steely Dan's "Rikki Don't Lose That Number," with a little techno thrown in.

But it was Nashville's own Ronnie Milsap. I'd know his gentle ballads anywhere. I got all teary and made the driver play the tape over and over for the rest of the trip. Ronnie Milsap enjoys unprecedented airplay throughout the remotest parts of Eastern Bhutan. A few years ago you could even buy his bootlegged tapes from Taiwan or Thailand at the market in a tiny town called Mongar, where red-robed monks and Bhutanese farmers chat and drink tea in front of shops. The Bhutanese love country music. They all know the words to "The Tennessee Waltz." There is even a musical instrument called the *dramyen,* a close cousin of the banjo, and I never feel very far from home when I hear it played.

Once, I cooked a dinner party for ten Bhutanese friends and made an all-Southern meal: fried chicken, mashed potatoes with milk gravy, corn bread, green beans cooked with bacon, pulled pork barbeque marinated in Jack Daniels, and Mississippi mud pie and banana pudding for dessert. A few of our guests were also marinated in Jack Daniels. They said it was the best food they had ever eaten, and even if they were just being polite, they ate like it was true.

In the U.S., we were both surprised by the excessive array of things in the stores, and by the large number of stores. Face it: we are over the top with stuff in America. In the suburb of Nashville where my parents lived, there were four very large grocery stores within a three-mile radius of their house. On top of that, they had two deep freezers in their garage. What did they need to freeze? Were the stores going to run out of food? Were they anticipating that all four of their legs would be broken at one time and they wouldn't be able to get to a store?

When Namgay and I went to his first American grocery store, he wandered around in amazement. He called my attention to a small, refrigerated bin of "specialty" cheeses at the front of the store. "Look at all that cheese!" he said.

"Wait," I said, taking him by the hand and leading him to the actual cheese section of the store—wall-to-wall cheese, stretching from the front all the way to the back of the store. "Look at all THAT cheese!" I said, lifting my arm in a flourish like I was presenting a prize on a TV game show. His mind was blown.

At the checkout, the clerk scanned our purchases. Namgay asked, "How does she know how much everything costs?"

"When she swipes the bar codes—those little black lines on the boxes and bags of food—over that little glass window on the checkout, it gives the prices," I said, sounding implausible even to myself.

"Plastic okay?" an attendant asked Namgay.

"Not so much," he replied.

"Yes," I said to the bag boy, "plastic's okay." And then to Namgay: "He's asking if we want our groceries in plastic bags."

"Then why didn't he say that?" Namgay asked.

"Actually, he did," I said.

As magical and strangely wonderful as I found Bhutan, so Namgay found the U.S. equally strange and wonderful. Taking him around the United States was like taking an awestruck, endangered snow leopard to Las Vegas. It reminded me of a movie I saw when I was a little girl, *Tarzan's New York Adventure*. In it, Jane and Tarzan follow Boy, their adopted son, to New York after an evil circus owner abducts him. Before hopping a plane to New York, they stop off at a Hong Kong tailor's (they came from Africa to the U.S. via Hong Kong?) to have a suit made for Tarzan. Tarzan is broad and muscular, accustomed to swinging in trees, so every time he tries on a coat he rips it down the back.

I thought of this in Bangkok, where Namgay had a suit made by a turbaned Sikh named Harry. Namgay was delighted to be getting his first suit. I taught him how to tie a Windsor knot and Namgay was transformed, at least physically, into a Western man.

Before we took the trip, he had never been on an elevator, eaten a hamburger, or enjoyed a chocolate milkshake. He'd never seen a vacuum cleaner, dishwasher, trash compactor, ATM, vending machine, car with automatic locks, or Western-style movie theater. He had never been to a shopping mall, ridden in a car on the Interstate, or traveled at over 40 miles an hour. He'd never seen a rodeo, the Metropolitan Museum of Art, or the Rubin Museum of Art in New York filled with Himalayan art, or drunk a single-malt scotch. Now he counts all of these marvels of Western culture as some of his favorite things.

"Only cars go on the American roads," Namgay observed. "Nobody walks or dries wheat on them." Bear in mind that Namgay is a man who saw his first car when he was eight years old. It came down the newly completed road near his village, and an old man tried to feed it.

He found American dogs to be extremely well behaved; American children, not so much. He was crazy about Walgreen's, Target, and The Sharper Image, where he could look for hours at the gadgets and appliances. He rarely wanted to own any of the stuff; he was happy just to look. Once, in a mall in Colorado, we spent two hours at a Sharper Image.

I had to coach him about how not to worry the security personnel. "Keep your hands out of your pockets and keep your coat unzipped," I said. "Don't pick up a lot of stuff!"

On that first visit we bought things like nail clippers, socks, and nice toothbrushes for everyone we knew in Bhutan. We were easily the most popular people in the country as a result.

The notion of choice also intrigued Namgay, since the limited number of items in any given shop in Thimphu precludes it. In a small shop in Thimphu you might find one tablecloth, one pair of underwear, and one pair of shoes that will fit you. Never mind that the shoes are a hideous green metallic: if the shoe fits, you must buy it—and wear it—even if it makes you look like a leprechaun.

Namgay, who grew up in the mountains of the Himalayas herding cows and sheep and being instructed by his Uncle Lama in religious rituals, was a devout Buddhist and an artist of some renown. But in the U.S., he became a devotee of appliances and worshipped on the altar of mass consumption.

He loved my parents' house, which is full of middle-class excess, namely appliances. The built-in vacuum system was a major source of amazement. I showed him the utility closet and the vacuum tube that hung on the wall, then how you could open the flap, jam the tube into the hole, and flick the switch, and the vacuum would start sucking. That's the last we saw of him. He was hooked.

I'd be sitting in the kitchen talking to my mother

and she'd say, "Where's Nam?" "Don't know," I'd answer. Then I'd hear the vacuum start in a room upstairs.

"I hope he doesn't wear out the rugs," she said.

On the way back to Bhutan, we bought a vacuum cleaner in Bangkok.

It was so much fun to see his face register surprise when he saw the ingenious packaging of Clorox Wipes that my mother kept in the bathroom closet and the way the next one would poke out of the slit in the top when you pulled one of the moist paper wipes out. He came into the bedroom one morning to show me the phenomenon as I was getting dressed. "We need some of these!" he said. I've never seen anyone get more pleasure from cleaning products.

He was stunned that almost every room in the house had a basket for trash tucked discreetly somewhere, lined with a white plastic bag, which was changed at intervals. In Bhutan, the few plastic bags we have are washed and hung out to dry and reused. Some of them have been around for years.

He'd take the trash out to the big bins in my parents' garage every day. But then reality hit and his face went dark. "Where does all this trash go?" he asked me. "To the dump," I said.

I could see he was doing the math: "Half the country must be the dump."

In Bhutan, we compost our vegetable waste and put plastic and paper waste into an ordinary-sized plastic garbage bin in our storeroom. Once every two or three months, when the bin is full, we drive it up to the dump about 20 minutes from our house. In the winter we use it to start fires in our woodstove. That is not to say that more waste isn't coming to Bhutan. But Bhutan, and the rest of the world for that matter, has a long way to go to catch up with the United States.

While enjoying the spectacle of Namgay's introduction to mass consumption, I was having reverse culture shock, having spent three years living in a world without appliances. I didn't watch television. We didn't have e-mail or Internet access. We didn't have a vacuum or dishwasher. When I told my mother we didn't have a washing machine, it made her cry. What I didn't tell her was that we didn't have a washing machine because half the time we didn't have running water, and we had to haul our water from outside in buckets.

Bhutan, however remote, was the home I shared with Namgay. I loved our visit to the U.S., but I was glad to go back to Bhutan. I asked Namgay what he liked most about the U.S.

"I love the ice and water that comes out of the door on the refrigerator," he said.

That's my man.

Soon after our trip, we got a television. It was an enormous 25-inch model that Namgay bought from a woman who worked at the UN office in Thimphu. She had finished her contract and was leaving the country and selling some of her stuff.

For a while, it was enough just to "have" a television, and it sat in the corner of the bedroom for almost a year before we bothered to plug it in and sign up for cable.

A few months later, we moved to a small house on a farm just outside of Thimphu. It had running water inside and the Thimphu River flowing next to it, screens on the windows, and toilets that flushed most of the time. In short, it was heaven on earth.

Insulation is a new concept in Bhutan, and there's no central heating, so most of the houses are cold in winter. Our house was not an exception. But the rest of the year the house was great. In summer, we opened all the windows and lived with the river noise, which is excellent for sleeping.

Namgay was not that enthusiastic about the place at first, because it was outside the town. He was afraid we would spend too much money on gas for the trip to and from Thimphu. We wanted to paint the house, and it needed a few repairs. But when we moved in, he really took to it. We had fun picking out Tibetan rugs at the weekend market, from smugglers who brought them into the country from China. We bought a few dishes that came from Bangladesh and several other things that the limited Thimphu market offered. Shopping was a new activity for Namgay. But his skills had been honed on our U.S. trip. He likes to shop; I enjoy watching him.

When he was young, nobody "shopped" in Bhutan. For one thing, there was nothing to buy. For another, nobody had any money.

"Where did you get your shoes?" I asked him one day.

"My father made them."

"From what?"

"He stitched deerskin."

His whole family wore moccasins made by his dad, and his mother wove their clothes. Sometimes I feel like I married the Last of the Mohicans. When he was a teenager, he helped his Uncle Lama with ceremonies, and occasionally people paid him in coins from India. His uncle saved the money for him until he had enough to buy some shoes when they went to Thimphu. That was in the late 1970s. He paid the equivalent of 60 cents for shoes from India.

Now Thimphu has many more items available for consumers than there were even a few years ago, and every year new ones are added. But there are no Targets, Walmarts, Home Depots, Costcos, or any large department stores in Bhutan. There are only tiny shops selling a limited selection of household items such as sheets, towels, and dishes. Everything has to be trucked in or flown in on Druk Air. The planes are tiny. Gas is expensive. What gets into Bhutan is self-limiting. A few pieces of furniture are imported from India or Thailand, but most people have their furniture made. You go to the local lumberyard and look at the furniture shown in an old IKEA catalog. You point to the table, chair, or bookcase you like, and then the woodworkers faithfully reproduce it. However, it's unlike IKEA furniture, because it's made in solid hardwood and is one-of-a-kind—for about a quarter of the price.

Namgay ordered several pieces of furniture for our house: a mirror, two cupboards, a worktable for me, and two small shelves. When they came, I gulped and then looked at the bill. I was stunned to see it was less than $200.

Over the years I've become adept at poking around the shops in Thimphu and finding the things we need. There isn't a vigorous mercantile system in Thimphu, so things will sit on the shelves of the stores for years. An item may collect dust or fall to pieces with age, but it will stay in the shop. Sometimes a shop will close and a new one will open up a few months later down the street. And you might see a lot of the merchandise from the old store in the new shop. Maybe it's the same proprietor, just a different location. Maybe the proprietor has packed it in and sold her stock to someone else.

The typical Thimphu shop is about eight feet square and has a very odd assortment of things: clothing from Nepal or Bangladesh—especially children's clothing and shoes, since there are a lot of children in Bhutan—could be mixed in with appliances, food, books, or sports paraphernalia. There are signs above the shops, as there are all over Thimphu, but they rarely describe reality. For example, you might see a sign that says "Pema Shop," in both English and Dzongkha, as required by law. The sign might also say "Shoes, Stationery, and Clothing"; and at one time, the shop owner might have intended to sell these very things. But maybe the shop changed hands, or the shoes, stationery, and clothing sold out and the owner decided to diversify. If you go into the shop, it's likely you won't see one shoe, one piece of clothing, or one sheet of paper—or Pema, for that matter. You may see rice, toothbrushes, and radios. It wouldn't occur to anyone to change the sign.

I have come to realize what I now perceive as a universal truth of merchandising: if you see something enough times, after a while it will grow on you. The line between revulsion and acceptance blurs, a kind of shopper's Stockholm Syndrome. For two years I passed a hideous ladies' polyester shirt, probably imported from India, hanging in the doorway of a shop. It was off-white with two very large green-and-orange urns, as in big vases, on the front of it. It was truly awful. Then one day I bought it. I wore it a couple of times, hoping someone would look at me and say, "Hey, nice jugs!" I'd clearly lost all perspective.

Cheap knock-off T-shirts are ubiquitous and reflect the ever-shifting zeitgeist. When I moved to Thimphu, a really hot item was a shirt with two ill-fated icons: the front of the shirt had an image from the movie *Titanic,* and the back had a head shot of Diana, Princess of Wales. For a while after that, it was Michael Jordan, then the Lakers logo. Now it's a mishmash of any and all things American. But the Japanese Hello Kitty is the most enduring of all images, even beating out Mickey Mouse.

What I love, and see more and more of, are formerly American images and slogans that the sweatshops of Asia have appropriated and made their own. For example, a shirt with an image of a big truck with stylized flames coming out the back of it. Instead of the words "Monster Truck" above the image, it might read "Monster Struck." I once saw a child wearing a T-shirt with an angel on the front and the words "I'm a Little Shithead" printed below. Somebody in a sweatshop in Asia is on familiar terms with irony.

There are dishes and pots from Thailand in the market—but hardly ever complete sets, only odd pieces. They must get broken on the way here. There are blankets, watches, shoes, and "silks" smuggled from China, very cheap and garishly colored, with a guarantee that the materials are man-made. There's nothing natural, as in cotton, wool, or silk. The display cases in the shops are filled with faux Louis Vuitton handbags, faux Christian Dior and Lancôme makeup, plastic combs, nail polish of every color, creams and lotions from India, shampoos, safety pins, candies, and cheap plastic jewelry, all crammed together.

We have a real developing-world motif in our home. We have beautiful, pricey Tibetan rugs under attractive lawn chairs from Thailand in our sitting room. In the dining room, a fake IKEA table and chairs of solid maple form our base for eating, doing homework, drinking tea, arguing, talking, and sitting around with friends. We have one of the few decent mattresses in the country, and it is our prized possession, but it's on the floor in our bedroom, as we haven't gotten a bed made for it yet.

About once a week, my friend Tara and I have a go at what she calls "The Boxes." Tara is a Bhutanese citizen but English born. She married the king's uncle back in the 1970s when very few people came into or out of Bhutan. She's raised three sons, one of whom is an actor in India. She has a wicked sense of humor and play that comes from being British and a true eccentric.

The Boxes are in several shops that have sprung up recently in Thimphu. Shopkeepers buy "seconds" from Bangladesh clothing factories in bulk—clothing with sleeves missing, broken zippers, or stains. The seconds are in rows and rows of big cardboard boxes, and we spend hours poring through them looking for amusement or bargains. Sometimes we find a gem, a pristine garment with no flaws.

"How's this?" I'll say to Tara, holding up a shirt I like with a small spot the color of coffee on the front.

"What look are you going for?"

"Decayed elegance. Do you think the spot will come out?"

"Maybe. Buy it and see."

One day I needed to send some letters to the U.S. Unlike shopping in the super-efficient States, getting the envelopes, stamps, and other stationery paraphernalia in Thimphu would take the better part of a day and a huge amount of focus and resolve.

There were two paper factories just next to the Riverview Hotel above the river road south of Thimphu. They were glorified shacks that seemed to defy gravity, like many buildings in Bhutan, by not sliding off a very steep hillock. As the tide of rural-to-urban migration swells, people are building higher and higher on these mountain slopes. When space is at such a premium, places that had previously been considered impossible to build on suddenly become plausible.

The word *factory* is misleading. Both paper outlets were tiny mud-walled buildings with a few small anterooms and a bigger room in the center, in which maybe five or six people were making exquisite handmade paper at their leisure.

Inside the first factory, the atmosphere was relaxed and friendly. The small showroom was filled with all shapes and sizes of paper. Great 24-by-16 sheets of white paper with marigold, poinsettia, and marijuana leaves imbedded in them were tempting, but I had a budget and a mission, so I declined the extravagance. I picked out 18 sturdy letter-sized envelopes and 11 slightly larger ones in a rough, natural-colored paper. It had the look of the cardboard that laundries in the U.S. fold cleaned shirts around, but it was lighter than air. The main ingredient of Bhutanese paper is bark from the Daphne tree. When the bark is pulled off the tree for paper, it regenerates, so Bhutanese paper, besides being beautiful, is eco-friendly.

As one man wrapped my small purchase—29 handmade envelopes for the equivalent of about $3—in beautiful paper that was also handmade, I chatted with the owner's son. We sat together on little stools in the factory and watched the workers. Someone brought us tea, which confirmed my theory that if you sit anyplace long enough in this country, someone will bring you a cup.

There were only three people working in the factory that day—two young men and an older woman. The older woman, dressed in a worn kira, sat on a stool next to a pile of pulp made from the bark, which she was shredding into smaller pieces. The pile was about four feet tall; and for half a second, it looked to me like a big pile of pork barbeque, which, in Tennessee, is also pulled. Even after more than ten years in Bhutan I have these kinds of delusional associations—remnants of my life in the U.S. I once saw what I swore was a village woman washing a barbecue grill in a river. I didn't catch what it really was, but I am absolutely certain it wasn't a grill.

Nearby, a man who looked to be in his late 20s stood at a waist-high wooden box on legs. It was full of pulp that had been boiled to the color and texture of porridge. With the graceful efficiency of someone who has done the same movement every day for years, he lowered a bamboo frame with a detachable bamboo mat on it into the pulp, shook it to spread the mixture and drain the excess water, then deftly flipped the bamboo mat over onto a pile of wet paper that sat on a low table. Water dribbled off the big tower of rectangular white sheets. The worker carefully peeled the mat away, leaving a single wet sheet, then dipped the bamboo frame in the pulp and repeated the process.

I watched the other worker peel individual layers of wet paper off a stack and smear them, one by one, onto four large, heated steel easels that quickly dried the sheets. His job was the most aerobic, because as soon as he finished loading the easel with four large sheets on either side, the first sheet was flat and dry and ready to take off. The drying easels were big, maybe eight feet long, and he had to work with some speed so the paper wouldn't singe.

I could have spent hours watching this obscure hive of activity, but I had more errands. These Bhutanese envelopes weren't going to seal themselves. They don't have adhesive, nor do the Indian ones we get. I went downtown to Lhaki Hardware, a shabby, ill-equipped place by American standards, but one of the best hardware stores in Thimphu. The front of the shop is filled to bursting with dusty Indian ropes, plastic, tin, wiring, sheeting, electrical sockets, cheap Indian space heaters from Siliguri, bathroom tiles, colorful stacked buckets, and other odds and ends. This unbelievably small space looks like a concrete bunker with a narrow door and three big windows. Four or five Indian men are always lounging about the place in plaid shirts and khaki pants. If you want something, say, a padlock, and it isn't visible in the front of the shop, one of the older men will bark something to one of the extremely wiry younger men, who will then disappear into the back of the shop and return, eventually, with what you need. Sometimes it's not in the back of the shop, and they just go down the street to another hardware shop for the item in question. Truth be told, many of the shop owners cherry-pick merchandise from each other.

Lhaki had cheap Indian glue I could use to seal the envelopes. Namgay had suggested that I also get some sealing wax to put on the back of the envelopes to make sure they stayed closed on the journey across the earth, Indian glue being occasionally unreliable. In this age of instant messaging, e-mail, texting, and the Internet, I loved the anachronism of sealing wax. The fact that it would be not only decorative but also practical thrilled me no end.

Lhaki didn't have any sealing wax, and none of the old men sent any of the younger men to get it. But I persevered, and three hardware shops later, on the upper market road, which has small shops owned by Tibetans, I found a new shop that had it. This place was small and crammed full of stuff, too. The proprietor climbed from shelf to shelf like a Chinese acrobat. He leapt from a stack of tires and grabbed a shelf high up in the rafters. I gasped. He looked like a human fly dangling in the shadows of the ceiling, which appeared to be about 12 feet high, moving along the shelf, peering into boxes and poking around with one hand while holding on with the other.

"Ah!" he cried. Success. He made his way down to earth, leaping onto the stack of tires, which swayed and nearly toppled as he landed on it. He quickly regained his balance and jumped onto a box, then onto the counter, to another box, and so to ground, one stick of red sealing wax in his hand.

He dusted off the wax with the sleeve of his gho and asked, "How many do you want?"

"Do you have more than one?" I inquired.

"I have a box," he said.

"How many sticks in the box?"

He didn't answer, but leapt onto the counter, the box, the tires, and finally up to the rafters again.

"Twenty," he yelled down.

"How much for the whole box?"

He looked at it, then looked at me. "Sixty ngultrum." About $1.50.

"I'll give you 50," I said.

He did the Indian bobble-head wag—as if his neck were a spring that attached his head to his shoulders. That meant yes.

With the box of sealing wax wrapped in an old newspaper, I crossed Norzin Lam, the main street, passed the traffic policeman in the kiosk in the middle of the street, and headed for the post office to get stamps. I was very close to being able to mail my letters.

The Thimphu Post Office occupies the right side of a large three-story building below the town, near the weekend vegetable market. Square and stately, white with the traditional red roof, it takes up a large chunk of prime real estate in the middle of Thimphu town. Bhutan National Bank—one of the three banks in Bhutan—occupies the left side of the imposing edifice; so it is a very social place, one where you are sure to meet many people you know standing out in front, chatting and enjoying the sun, or doing their banking inside the dark building.

The post office's stamp room has display cases of old, out-of-print stamps and commemorative envelopes lining the walls, and two glass display cases on one side, also filled with commemorative stamps and gift books. Everything is for sale. For about 20 years, from the mid-1960s to the mid-1980s, revenue from postage stamps for collectors made up about a quarter of Bhutan's GNP; it still makes up a large portion of the country's GDP, and Bhutan still issues some of the most beautiful and unusual stamps the world has ever seen. They reproduce exquisite Japanese prints and European Old Masters in stamps. Some stamps commemorate world leaders and events: there are 3D stamps of the lunar landing, Gandhi, Princess Diana, and American astronauts. There are Yeti stamps, stamps which are CD-ROMs that play the Bhutanese national anthem, and silk stamps. There are dragons, flowers, yak, birds, and Buddhas.

I had saved the post office for last because I always lose track of time looking at stamps. It is satisfying in the extreme to turn the pages of the enormous ledger books filled with gorgeous stamps, pull whole sheets out of the plastic sleeves, and tear off the ones you want. There are several hundred different stamps from which to choose, and I can never stop myself from getting more than I need.

The post office is also a popular destination for tourists. On this particular day, I was hoping that I wouldn't encounter a tour group, especially a German one. Germans really hog the stamp books and take a long time to decide. Japanese are quick, impulsive stamp buyers and will share the big books with you. Americans are sometimes stamp hoggers, too.

Luckily, I was alone. My friend Pema, the stamp-room attendant, greeted me and we chatted in Dzongkha as I made my selections. She speaks English, but somehow we've gotten into the habit of speaking Dzongkha to each other. My broken syntax and baby diction are guaranteed to give her a laugh.

I picked out beautiful stamps with dragons. Then I couldn't resist a series of six stamps commemorating American astronauts. There were also some silver and black holographic stamps featuring the space shuttle that I had to have, and some yak stamps.

Pema made a phone call to the postal canteen, below the main floor, and a peon brought two steaming cups of tea with milk and sugar. It was my fourth cup that day. Shopping makes me drink a lot of tea. I sat with Pema behind the counter until a guide brought in two cheerful elderly American tourists who bought about $400 worth of stamp gift books for their grandkids. I'd run out of money, so I couldn't pay Pema for the stamps. She kindly said I could bring the balance—about $5—some other time. We didn't have credit cards at that time in Thimphu, but we did have credit.

It was already 3 P.M. I was hungry for lunch, and it was time to go home. I needed some nice bond paper to write on, but that would have to wait for another day.

On the way home, I thought of the time I'd bought envelopes with Namgay in Nashville. We had only been there for a day and a half. Still jet-lagged and fuzzy and feeling like alien beings that had landed on earth from some other planet, we went to an Office Depot with my father. The size of the place and the enormous range of choices made us feel sleepy and jittery at the same time. I asked my father to take us to a smaller store without so many choices. He thought I was nuts. I was dangerously close to a panic attack, and Namgay was becoming delusional. How could we decide on 100, 200, or 500 envelopes? Did we want acid-free? Dubl-Vue? Parchment? Recycled? Double Window? Multi-Use? Self Seal? Security? Clean-Seal Security? White Weave? #10? #9? Cotton Resume Mailing? Fine Business Envelopes? Security Tint?

It's the reverse of what Westerners who come to Bhutan experience, but the feeling is similar. They think: *How do people live in Bhutan with so little convenience and so little to choose from? How do they manage with nothing in the shops and no adhesive on their envelopes?* On the other hand, I defy anyone in the U.S. to stop what he or she is doing and go out and buy 29 individual handmade envelopes directly from the maker. I'm sure you have to look really hard. I'm not sure it can be done. If it can, then it's difficult—and expensive.

If you stay in a place long enough, eventually it

becomes familiar. Likewise, with enough time and distance, things that were once familiar become wildly exotic. After living ten years in Bhutan, I find the tables have turned. Shopping in the U.S. seems insane.

Namgay says the grocery stores in the U.S. look like temples.

"What do you mean, they look like temples? They *are* temples," I tease.

Wisdom is having things right
in your life and knowing why.

— **WILLIAM STAFFORD,** *THE LITTLE WAYS*
THAT ENCOURAGE GOOD FORTUNE

A PERFECT
UNION

It's late fall, and our house turns cold when the sun goes down, so we go to bed early.

The way we live, the inside temperature is pretty close to the outside temperature. There are large gaps between the windows and the walls, and if I put a stack of papers on the dining-room table in the morning, by late afternoon most of the papers will be on the floor. We dress in layers. A kira feels wonderful in winter; it's like wearing a blanket.

The garden has gone to seed and flocks of birds stop to refuel at the paddies across the river on their way south to India. I take walks in the afternoon. I've found a lovely place at a bend in the river. I hike through our neighbor's land to get there, but he doesn't mind. It's a 20-minute walk from my house to the spot, past the neighbor's traditional three-story white house, past delicate terraces of recently harvested paddy. Now the ground is hard and cracked; and there are yellow-brown stems of rice, like dead grass.

139

A dirt lane parallels the river, and I pass the cowboy's ever-expanding hut. He's an actual "cow" boy, as opposed to a Marlboro man, in that he takes care of our neighbor's cows. He has a wife and two children now, so he needs more space. He has recently had his house wired for electricity; this means he has a television. I can see it flickering through the window. A cow is looking in his window; it looks like she's watching television, too.

Two gates and the remains of a cornfield and I am at the river. I sit on a tuft of thick dead grass above the round river rocks with the white noise of the river to listen to and the warm winter sun on my back. It is a heaven of the senses, optimal for emptying my mind. To have an empty mind you have to dump everything. For a while my mind races as everything comes to the surface.

This little spot I have come to think of as my hideout. Living in Bhutan is already like hiding out from the rest of the world, so here I suppose I'm about as far away from the world as I can get without leaving the planet, a hideaway within a hideaway. I recommend two things to anybody interested in finding out more about who they really are, what they're made of, what they can endure, and how far humor will take them: running away and hiding out. If you have a chance to do either or both in your life, then by all means take it.

Two trees at the bend in the river act as camouflage. Some people might call what I'm doing meditation, but I prefer the term daydreaming. It is a lost art.

I look around. Everything is achingly beautiful, shining in the pristine air. The glorious early-winter light; the river, now bright blue reflecting the sky; whitecaps, perfect in their water-ness—these white flecks of pure liquid energy make me feel relaxed.

I think of the movie *White Mischief* and the character that actress Sarah Miles plays, a jaded American heiress living in Kenya. Every morning she opens the French doors in her bedroom and views the spectacular Kenyan landscape, the flawless sky, and says, "Oh, God, not another fucking beautiful day." I don't want to be jaded by this beauty.

The water is rushing and so clear you can see the smooth black and brown rocks shimmering at the bottom. In fact, everything shimmers. The thin air is crisp and electric. A haze in the distance will burn off in an hour or so. Hot sun high up takes the edge off, so it's not that cold. The brush-covered cliff to my right had bear tracks below it a few weeks ago. The bears were foraging, getting ready to hibernate. Above, the tree line goes all the way up a small slope to the sky. The landscape is one-third blue sky, two-thirds sand and evergreen trees pointing up, taking my eyes to heaven. Nearby, green and red prayer flags on long poles whip gently in the wind, sending prayers off to the cosmos.

I envision myself growing roots like a tree. My legs knot at the place where they meet the ground, my buttocks grow long roots that push into the earth. My straight spine forms one long brown taproot that burrows down into the ground as it forms fine lateral rootlets. I am immovable and unyielding.

Rivers figure largely in my personal metaphors: water coming and going means being graceful, fluid, and adaptable. *Learn to be water.* In dreams, rivers are symbols of change or transition. The river we live next to, the one I sit beside, is called the Thimphu Tsang Chu, or Clean River. If the water weren't so cold, newly melted from the glacier, I'd wade in and lie down in it, have a baptism. Instead, I take a handful and shock my face.

One laughing redstart, a tiny cobalt-blue bird with a bright red tail, skims the surface of the water to catch a bug and flies off into the trees. He's staying late in the season.

I'm aware how far away the world is from this maze of rivers cutting through mountains. I can't stop thinking of this as an impossible place, as magical. It's certainly done its magic on me, and I feel like a benevolent Buddha.

Of course, I am far from Buddha-like. I am very much of the world, and stressed. That's why I've come to the river. I like to unwind here because even in Bhutan the world closes in. There are things to do, hassles, and tensions, and we're always broke. But here we live so much in the moment. It's a gift to know this: that life and the world are fleeting, like water in a river. Knowing that change is inevitable and life is ephemeral is being mindful. It makes each moment rich with possibilities. To really understand this, to feel it, you have to derail, switch off, and run away. That's why I come here.

Today the sun is blinding until my eyes get used to the light. Semtokha Dzong sits off in the distance, as if it has floated down out of the sky to perch on the side of the hill and rest. Dreamy, wispy clouds are coming off the mountains. It's practically cinematic. I have an image of a camera crew—maybe 50 people with lights and wind machines and lots of equipment—just out of my line of vision. Someone yells, "Cue the clouds!" Then a big vat of dry ice is uncovered and they switch on a wind machine and the clouds float up.

The dzong is picturesque, surrounded by a cedar grove, like a fairy castle. It's built in the typical Bhutanese style, white with red trim and the red-and-yellow roof that signifies a temple or holy place. It's big enough to house a thousand monks. Smoke comes out of a pocket in the pine trees. Has someone built a fire? Some hardwoods are already golden. Others, far in the distance near the cerulean sky, look like the backs of funny green beasts in profile. The river babbling along is taking all the tension out of my body. *I should have come here days before. I should never leave.*

It's almost winter, my favorite season. I know this is unusual. I love the way the trees have a soft brown look without their leaves. *In a few weeks.* Winter is an inward time. Trees abandon their leaves, and their sap, their life force, concentrates in the trunks. The river makes a soft lulling sound, a winter sound; and water moves slowly, like it is caught up in the sunlight and wants to stay. *Slow glistening of the sun on the slow-moving water. A clean sound.* Here, my body rooted to the earth, my thoughts flowing, I understand that we can't see what's right in front of us unless it is comfortable and expected. To truly see something, we don't need to rely on senses: taste, touch, smell, sight, hearing. For clear perception, we need to rely more on natural, not reasoned, impulses.

I think of the choices I've made in my life. For me, there is a big difference between choosing and deciding: Choosing means we take the initiative—we learn about options, think of alternatives, and then pick one—and I prefer it. Deciding means someone has already made the choices for us. They are assembled in front of us, like a big menu in a fast-food restaurant. We merely pick A, B, or C. It is more passive. These aren't the traditional dictionary definitions of choosing and deciding I'm using, but I make the distinction because in the world, so many things seem to be decided for us. We don't really believe we have much choice. But we do.

If we choose to follow our dreams and desires, then other things, good or bad, fall into place. I discovered this in Bhutan. In its remotest corners, with so many layers stripped away, I find my inside self is the same as my outside self.

Pemagatshel (pronounced Pem-ah-GOT-sill) is a far-flung province of southeastern Bhutan near the border with India. I went there on a visit in 1996. Here, the Himalayas begin to flatten out and smooth into hills; they level even more at the border, like a rumpled tablecloth someone has pulled tight and smoothed, and become great river deltas called the Duars, or "gates." This is prime farmland. But the spoils of Pemagatshel's modest fields never reach the markets of Thimphu or of Guwahati, the capital of Assam, the Indian state that borders Bhutan, because there are too many mountains and rivers between and not enough roads. So the farmers are poor and only grow enough to feed their sparsely populated communities of people and livestock. The women help with farm work, tend to the children, and dye and weave a highly prized homespun linen called *bura*. In the growing season, they spend their days and nights keeping wild pigs from eating their crops and tigers from killing their horses and cattle, and they take turns sleeping in huts they've constructed in the fields so they can chase away vermin. Life is about survival, with a little rest at the end of the day if they're lucky. At the new year, they perform pujas to thank the powers that be and ask for protection, good health, and safekeeping for all they love; and if it's not too much trouble, just one more year of good crops and nice steady rains to make them grow. They have no knowledge of the rest of the world.

I hired a friend, Tenzin, to drive, and we stayed with his many relatives as we traversed the country. Outside of

Trashigang, in the far eastern part of the country, the universal joint on his dilapidated old Toyota broke. But our luck was good: he had a relative with a blowtorch in nearby Khaling who patched it in a day and sent us on our way.

Near the end of the trip, we came to an old house in Pemagatshel full of four generations of his kin. I got out of the car and was ushered into a tidy little bedroom that doubled as the family's temple room, then shown a seat on the bed in front of an old television that looked like it had been through a war. A small boy switched it on, put a cassette in an ancient videocassette deck, and left. A young girl brought me a cup of tea. It was truly the royal treatment: electricity and access to a movie and a television screen meant these folks were well off. I was treated to a Chinese kickboxing movie from the early '70s (judging from the length of the actors' sideburns). If they hadn't had a TV, I'd have been handed a photo album filled with faded pictures of friends and family on picnics or on pilgrimages to India.

I settled back, awaiting the onslaught of food, but after a moment there was yelling far off in the distance. I went to the window. In a far field, over a rise, an archery match was going on.

All over Bhutan, teams of men, 12 to a team, compete in daylong, sometimes weekend-long, archery tournaments. Rich, poor, fat, thin, handsome, ugly, old, young, sober, high—all Bhutanese men love archery. The players shoot at targets on either side of a playing field that are an impossible 150 yards away; the targets are tiny markers only about six inches wide. It is remarkable that the archers can see them, much less hit them.

Someone had made a bull's-eye, and the archers of his team were doing the victory dance, which is akin to a slow-motion Highland reel; and singing a rough, loud victory song. It was late afternoon, so it was reasonable to assume most or all of the participants were drunk.

Separated by distance and a windowpane, I watched. Inside the house was warm, and the late-afternoon sun made the outside look yellow and dreamy with long black shadows.

Tenzin came to see how I was doing. Attentive, respectful, but always ironic, he said, "Shall I go and ask the men to be quiet so you can hear the movie?"

"Why do Bhutanese love archery so much?" I asked.

"They like to throw things at things."

I laughed. "I love Bhutan," I said.

"I know," he said. "You are the arrow that has hit its mark."

Now, years later, outside of Thimphu, I understand that back then in Pemagatshel I was responding to that genuineness, that quality of life when you strip it down to the basics. Happiness can't be willed. You have to get in the right situation and then let it come to you. I learned this by living in Bhutan.

Most evenings after dinner Namgay and I sit and talk to each other. He tells me the most wonderful stories of his life in Bhutan before we met. I sit and listen, then sneak away, on the pretext of making coffee, to make notes so that later I can write the stories down.

Occasionally the electricity goes off. We light candles and sit together in the living room. If it's cold, we get a blanket and wrap up together. One night in July, shortly after we moved to our house, we went outside after dinner and sat in the garden and watched the stars.

Since Thimphu is a mile above sea level and the air is very clear, we can see millions of stars, along with thousands of satellites that orbit the earth.

I sat with Namgay on a little cane sofa, my head in his lap, looking up at the stars, and he told me the story of Baje and the two pigs.

Baje worked in the Painting School canteen as assistant cook for over 20 years. From the time he was 12 years old, he came every day to the shack that served as the kitchen. He'd collect the firewood and start a big fire at about 5:30 A.M. Around 6, while he was stirring the big aluminum vat of butter tea, the students would arrive to wash their faces in the tap outside the kitchen. They laughed and joked with each other and paid no attention to Baje. They brought their cups on sunny mornings, cold mornings, and rainy mornings, and he ladled out their tea.

By 6:30 he'd cleaned the rice and had it boiling on the fire in a big vat. Thirty or so students would eat nearly 30 pounds of rice every day, so he was always cleaning rice, cooking rice, stirring big tubs of it, or cleaning the pots.

The walls of the shack were black with soot from the fires and gave off the starchy smell of rice. Sometimes student helpers would come to make *eazyee*—chopped onion, tomato, salt, and chili—which the students would eat for breakfast with rice. After the morning meal, it was time for Baje to start peeling potatoes for lunch. On rare occasions there would also be vegetables to chop for a curry to eat with the rice. On very special occasions there would be a little meat. Baje spoke very little, went on with his work, and paid no attention to the students as he fed them. They were learning to be craftsmen, painting thankas, carving wood and stone, and weaving. In

Bhutanese society, craftsmen are quite low; there is little status associated with working with the hands. But they are more upwardly mobile than cooks or their assistants, so the students were a grade up from Baje. As a result, and because they were kids, some of them liked to tease and belittle him. But he said nothing. He took their jokes good-naturedly, laughing along with them when they called him "boy" or "monkey," even though he was older than they. His day ended around 8 P.M., after he'd finished washing the big pots of food from the evening meal and setting up for the next day. He then made his way home to the shack where he lived. Since there was no electricity, he lit a candle and a small fire, drew water from a nearby stream, and washed as well as he could. He said his evening prayers and dropped into bed. This is the way he lived every day for almost 20 years.

When Baje was 30, one of the old men from his village came to Thimphu and Baje ran into him in the vegetable market. Baje had a bit more status than this village man because of his cooking job and because he lived in Thimphu. The man asked Baje if he wanted to marry his daughter. Baje had never considered taking a wife. He barely made enough money to buy shoes, much less support a wife and the inevitable children that would come.

He declined as graciously as he could and offered to buy the man a beer. They went to a hotel nearby, and one beer became three, then five. The village man reiterated his offer to give his daughter in marriage to Baje, but this time he sweetened the deal: he offered Baje two baby pigs he'd brought to sell in the weekend market. This time Baje accepted.

Baje's wife was several years his senior and difficult to look at. In her teens she'd run away with a soldier and been abandoned by him in another village four days' walk from her own. When she came back, her father, in a rage, slashed her face with his razor. Now, the daughter was spoiled not only by the "temporary marriage," but also by the scar on her once pretty face and an eye that was always red and weeping.

But she was a good woman, and she never complained about the one-room shack where Baje took her to live. She kept it clean and washed his clothes and kept to herself instead of drinking tea all day and chatting as the other wives in the neighborhood did.

She hauled wood from the forests above the city and water from the stream near the house. She repaired the wood of the house when the wind and rain made holes, and she covered the inside with bits of newspaper when it was cold in the winter. She weaved ghos for Baje to wear and kiras for herself. Occasionally she made some extra and sold them in a local shop to add to the family income.

The two piglets lived in the house with them. There was no other place for them until Baje was able to fashion a small pen next to his house. Anyway, they were valuable, so they couldn't be left outside to wander away or get stolen. Every day Baje brought the scraps from the students' meals to feed the pigs. Every morning Baje's wife would get up and boil the slop brought home the day before to feed the pigs. Sometimes there wasn't enough, so he'd feed them some or all of the food his wife had cooked for him. In summer Baje picked armloads of the marijuana that grew wild in the field above his house and fed it to the pigs. This made them fat and happy. They grew bigger and pinker every day.

The Painting School students would come round to Baje's little house next to the school's kitchen to poke fun. "Hey, pig man!" they'd shout, and they'd push their noses up to look like pigs. "Come out and show us your ugly snout." Baje paid no attention.

Two years later, in the spring, the pigs were ready for slaughter. Baje asked the head cook if he could take two weeks' leave from his job, and the cook agreed. Baje found a butcher to kill the pigs and borrowed a cart to haul the meat to the weekend market. He sold the meat within a few hours and made about $200.

This was better than he'd expected. The people in Thimphu had just finished a holy month and the supply of meat was low. So the pig meat went quickly and for a good price.

He bought himself a bus ticket for about $2, and took the six-hour trip to Phuentsholing, on the Indian border. Phuentsholing was flat compared to Thimphu. It sat at the very bottom of the Himalayas on a riverbed at the beginning of the Duars Plain. As the bus wound along the mountain roads, nearing Phuentsholing, Baje could see the wide plains of India dotted with tea plantations and cut by rivers that poured out of the mountains and became tributaries. The world looked vast.

That night he ate some rice and *dal,* or lentil stew, his wife had packed for him and slept under a tree in the park at the center of the town. He had never been so far from home. The next day he took most of the pig money and bought clothes: socks, sport shirts, track pants, and pieces of cloth. He bargained hard with the merchants of Phuentsholing and the neighboring Indian town of Jaigon to get as much as he could. It was his life savings.

Baje wrapped the clothes with pieces of rope and took the bus back to Thimphu. But he didn't go home. He bought another bus ticket, this time to Punakha, two hours east of Thimphu over the Dochula Pass. When the bus reached Punakha, Baje set off walking to the northwest, to the village of Talo, about three hours away in the mountains above the town. He hadn't eaten since the night before in Phuentsholing and his bundle of clothes was very heavy, so the walk took four hours instead of three. But Baje knew that he could rest a bit in Talo and that the people of Talo, being Bhutanese, wouldn't let him go hungry, so he pressed on.

In Talo village he was met by laughing children who were awed by the sight of a strange man with a large bundle strapped to his back. They followed him as he made his way to the gup's house. The gup's house was easy to spot. It was the nicest house in the village, freshly painted in the Bhutanese way, bright whitewash with elaborate animals and flowers covering the outside walls. He waited outside until someone came to the door and invited him in. Without speaking, he went inside and untied the bundle of clothes. Someone brought him a cup of tea and some *zow*, rice baked in the sun. Several women came into the room and began to examine the clothes. Soon the room was filled with men, women, and children poring over the clothes. Some were ready with cash. Some offered rice, salt, or chickens in lieu of cash for the Indian clothes he'd bought in Phuentsholing.

In this way he halved the bundles of clothes, going from house to house in the village. If the people had no money he bartered for rice or salt. He borrowed a horse from one of the men in the village and took his clothes and food to Lobesa, then to the next village over. There he sold the remainder of the clothes. With about $300 and about 150 kilograms of rice, a few chickens, and some salt, he returned to Punakha, left the horse for its owner, and took the bus back to Thimphu. In Thimphu he sold the rice, chickens, and salt at the weekend market. He'd doubled his money from the sale of the pig meat with the clothes he'd bought in Phuentsholing and the food he'd bartered them for in the villages. He went home long enough to bathe, eat, and give his wife a piece of cloth he'd bought her in Phuentsholing to make herself a tdego.

Then he did it all over again. He took the bus down to Phuentsholing, bought about $400 worth of clothing in the bazaar, and brought it back to Thimphu. This time he headed toward Ha, about four hours west. He rented a horse in Ha village and set about selling the clothes in small villages between Paro and Ha. Again, those not able to pay in cash were encouraged to pay with rice or other commodities.

Back at the weekend market in Thimphu, the people were happy to buy the barley and rice from Ha. At the end of the day Baje had over $2,000 in his purse. He staggered home and slept for two days without waking.

Ten days after he'd sold the pig meat, Baje went to the High Court to visit a man he knew from his village. "I want to buy some land," Baje told the man. The man laughed and offered him some doma. Baje reached into the front of his gho and pulled out the purse with the money in it. The man stopped laughing.

The man, Sonam Phuntsho, took Baje on the back of his scooter to Hejo, a little village east of Thimphu near the king's palace. They came to a large rice paddy of about two acres. "This land is for sale," said Sonam. "You have enough money." Baje and Sonam took an hour or so and walked the perimeter of the property without speaking.

"I'll take it," Baje said. They went into Thimphu to have a meal to celebrate. At the Wangdue Hotel, Sonam and Baje ordered rice, dal, kewa datsi—potatoes, chilies, and cheese—and chicken curry. Baje bought a beer for every guest at the hotel, three men and one woman. He and Sonam shared a bottle of Special Courier, a locally brewed scotch. "I want to build a house," said Baje. "If you help me, I'll give you half my land and you can also build yourself a house."

It took several months for the paperwork to go thought the court, but Baje and Sonam were already collecting wood and stone to build two houses, one for each of them, on the property. By the time the property was registered in Baje's name, they'd built a shed to store the building materials.

Sonam went to Jaigon, and hired nine Indian laborers from Cooch Behar. The men of Cooch Behar are known for their carpentry skills and will work in Bhutan for about $1.50 a day. This is three times the wage they'd get in India, so they have been coming to Bhutan to work for generations. In eight months the laborers had built two small, neat houses on the property. Baje and his wife and Sonam Phuntsho and his family live in these houses.

Now, when the Painting School students see Baje at the weekend market, they bow and call him "sir."

Even now, the story of Baje has a profound effect on me. The charm of it; the simplicity; the goodness and focus of Baje; his Herculean, earnest efforts; and his wonderful success reminded me of Namgay's life—of any life that is hard won. So many Bhutanese have stories like this. I realized what I'd married into was epic, and also worthy of tremendous respect.

Baje's story made me acutely aware of the difference between how we think in the West and in a place like Bhutan. It is a reminder of what is important here: life is about improving yourself and your lot. It sounds simple, but it's really not. There is a great deal of physical and mental energy expended. But the people I know and love here don't judge themselves to be optimistic or pessimistic, or tenacious, or creative, or ruthless, or any of these labels. Life is not about thinking and reasoning and rationalizing—it's about intent and the subsequent action. Ancient traditions still dictate; life here is, more than anything, about what you aim for.

The wind as I sit beside the river has whipped up and is wild, making itself known. It blusters through the trees and throws up dust. The wind is a force that some in Bhutan claim carries spirits. At the very least, it signals the change of season. The cows munching on dead grass on the hillside don't seem to notice that the wind is so fierce it might blow them away. On a knoll where there is no grass, it stirs up dust devils, sucking up stray leaves in the minitornadoes. I cover my eyes with my hand until it subsides. Living here, I understand the notion of time as a quality or shade of being. We are ruled by weather, so time is inseparable from the seasons, what food we eat, where we go, what we do. We are able to forget about the schedules of the world for now and make a little world of our own. Sit back and take care of our own.

The river changes color from hour to hour, depending on the light and the weather. In the short time I've been sitting here, mare's-tail clouds have formed, blowing high above the mountaintops. There is a faint smell of pine.

I've been sitting with my eyes closed. Sometimes I fear that if I blink or tilt my head a certain way, all the beauty of Bhutan, these gorgeous evergreen mountains dotted with fall foliage, the white snowcaps in the distance, will disappear. *Mindful of being mindful. Change is the constant. Suffering inevitable. Sow your own garden.*

If enlightenment is possible anywhere, I think it is particularly possible here. Tantric Buddhism teaches that there are many paths—as many as there are stars in the sky. Vajrayana, the diamond vehicle, means that anything can be an aid to enlightenment: jade, meditation, coq au vin, standing still, sex, walking out of a door, compassion, waking up, happiness, intuition, choosing, not taking yourself so seriously, mountains, breathing.

Like the title character in Voltaire's *Candide: Or Optimism,* the 18th-century satire about how we ought to view the world, I'm a disenchanted optimist. Most optimists are, when they reach a certain age or accrue enough experiences. Dr. Pangloss, Candide's teacher, said, "This is the best of all possible worlds." This is not true. Yet I do believe in miracles and magic in this part of the world. I believe in accidental enlightenment. It could happen, and probably about as easily as one could become enlightened from, say, reading a lot of books about Buddhism.

Once Namgay told me that in Gida, the next valley over toward Paro, there was an 18th-century cross-dressing libertine Buddhist lama named Wang Drugay. He was a big, important holy man, a high reincarnate, so everybody had to put up with him.

I suppose at the time the valleys were full of populist holy men. Wang Drugay was fond of dressing up like a nun so he could live at the nunneries and have sex with the nuns. No, really.

One of the nuns became pregnant. The nunnery was off-limits to men, so the abbess correctly deduced that a man had infiltrated their number. In an attempt to smoke him out, both literally and figuratively, she ordered a fire to be built for a ceremony and made all the nuns jump over the fire in a purging ritual. They had to hike their robes up so they wouldn't catch fire. She figured it would be easy to spot the man.

Wang Drugay tied a string to his penis and testicles, ran it up his back, and secured it around his neck, thereby hiding his privates between his legs. When it was his turn to jump over the fire, the fire singed the string and his privates came down for all to see. Everyone was shocked, except the nuns he'd been sleeping with, who just *acted* like they were shocked.

I'd heard this story before from other people. The Bhutanese love Wang Drugay, and anybody who gets away with stuff or beats the system. Bhutan is where the iconoclasts of the world have reincarnated.

The stories of Baje and Wang Drugay, as well as my own journey from West to East, remind me that all of us, in our own way, on our own terms, just want to be happy, just want to be better, and this is profound. They also make me think that happiness and achievement probably look very different to each of us.

I feel lucky to live in a place where Gross National Happiness is a radical social experiment. This decision by the government to pursue happiness helps instill in Bhutan's people an immense sense of well-being that infuses everything here. I also have the good luck to have come from a place, the U.S., where capitalism reigns supreme. It's still one of the richest countries in the world, and life is pretty good. I am well situated to compare the two philosophies of living.

People do most everything, in a capitalist society, to get money. What they forget is that they want money because they want to be happy. I didn't see this clearly, or see how insidiously our entrepreneurial social system permeates everything, until I lived in a place where people made decisions that weren't based just on economics.

The Bhutanese are not very good at making money, but they are happier than Americans.

I like that I can have it both ways. I know how it is to be American, and it's fun chasing my tail sometimes, and even in these post-9/11, end-of-history times, it's still a great country. I also love being lost in Bhutan.

Since we're all trying to be happy, and since I've studied happiness in depth for some time, I feel qualified to make some observations:

There will probably be some physical pain and some form of renunciation on the road to happiness. No, I'm not advocating masochism. But once you take the road to happiness—the road less traveled, or the open road, or whatever you envision as your route to bliss—you have to be ready to face some discomfort. Ironically, this will make you happier. Try to avoid associating happiness with comfort.

We are hopelessly addicted to comfort in the U.S. I submit that comfort is a diversion, and it's not related to happiness. We have plenty to eat, and though this should afford us some comfort, it doesn't really. As we collectively loosen our belts and try to touch our collective toes, we realize we're not happy. We're too fat. We're unhealthy. So we go buy some more stuff. And maybe on the way home from the mall we get something to eat.

It's not just physical comfort we're addicted to. We are addicted to insulating ourselves from unpleasant realities. The average Bhutanese knows much more about the world than the average American and goes through some discomfort, if you will, or at the very least some maneuverings, to pay attention to what's going on. Bhutan is small, fragile, and vulnerable. It behooves the people of Bhutan to know their adversaries and to keep tabs on what's happening in the rest of the world. Americans don't feel that urgency. What we learn when we do look beyond our shores is uncomfortable and disconcerting. It's more comfortable to watch fake news about celebrities than to know what's happening in China or Southern Sudan. But events happening in China or Sudan affect us so much more because they are real.

It's an old story. John Donne said, "No man is an island, entire of itself; every man is a piece of the continent, a part of the main. . . . Any man's death diminishes me, because I am involved in mankind; and therefore never send to know for whom the bell tolls; it tolls for thee."

And it is even more true now than it was in 1624 when Donne wrote it. We have more, bigger, ways, for better or worse, to connect to and influence each other in the world. It may be uncomfortable or unpleasant, but we have to cultivate some awareness of what's happening to the rest of the world, and we have to actively participate in each other's lives.

Renunciation follows the desire for happiness naturally, but in our national disconnect, we can no longer intuit that small is beautiful and less is more. The inclination of Americans is to pile it on, get more, supersize, acquire: larger houses, bigger pants and bigger cars, more gadgets, another piece of cake—and eat up more of the ozone while you're at it. Our recent economic problems drive home the point. The way we live is unsustainable. Now we're all beginning to see.

Giving up, letting go, pushing away, peeling off, and culling will make you happier. I know you don't believe this. But answer this question: How happy are you now with all your stuff? Are you blissful? Will a set of new towels make you blissful? If so, for how long?

Another truth about happiness is this: *Ultimately, no one else can make you happy. You have to do it for yourself.* But you know this already. If other people make you happy, then great—it's value added. But we put way too much pressure on our loved ones when we make them responsible for our happiness. Which leads to my last point: *Happiness doesn't come from outside forces. It comes from how you view the outside forces. It comes from inside.* In other words, attitude is everything. You can train yourself, like your mom trained you to wash your hands before meals, to have an attitude that is conducive to happiness.

The first thing you do is think about death. Several times a day. This will clarify a lot for you. It's a shortcut, because, in the end, so much of what we do is to avoid thinking about our end, so focusing on it will help you stabilize your mind. A stable mind won't make you happy, but it will set the stage for happiness. Next, just like you train your mind to think about death, so you can train it to manifest gratitude. If you have two arms and two legs, be grateful for them. If not, be grateful for the air you breathe, and then take a good deep breath. Look for other things to be grateful about; be grateful you're alive.

159

A place where there isn't any trouble.
Do you suppose there is such a place Toto?
There must be. It's not a place you can get
to by a boat or a train. It's far, far away.
Behind the moon, beyond the rain.

— DOROTHY, *THE WIZARD OF OZ*

Chapter 10

CEREMONY

A big part of life in Bhutan is giving thanks, and traveling a long way to do it. In fact, the more distance and difficulty, the more karmic points you accrue. It's May; and we're on our way to a puja in Bumthang and the car is loaded with food, gifts, bedding, a tent, and everything else we need to make a trip cross-country. When people travel in Bhutan they have to take a lot with them. It's not like there are Holiday Inns at regular intervals. In fact, there's nothing at regular intervals.

While Namgay drives, I relax. He's chanting a prayer for safety and it lulls me, as does the bright sun and the rhythm of the car as he maneuvers it left and right. As we wind through the mountains, I'm hypnotized like a snake by the charmer's flute. The road has about 30 hairpin turns per mile, or a turn every nine seconds; so it seems like you're never actually moving forward. But thanks to some perversity of my DNA, I love the feeling of being lost in some far-flung spot. I've always liked traveling by road, the more obscure the better. Summers of my childhood I went to Central and South America to visit my grandparents at their various postings. My grandfather, a road engineer, must have had a similar desire to get lost. In Nicaragua, he went by helicopter to a clearing in the jungle to view the progress of a future road, and as he circled in the big bird, the villagers, blasted by the rotors' wind, hacked out a perimeter in the tall grass for it to land. Being stuck in the mud in the Philippine jungle and traveling by convoy outside of Tehran prepares one for life on the obscure, untraveled road. And none is more obscure than in Bhutan. The car lurches as Namgay takes another hairpin turn at about 20 miles an hour and my thoughts start and stop like the little bird, a redstart, that's flitting in front of our car.

"Why do those little birds always fly in front of the car?" I ask Namgay.

"They're trying to lead us away from their nests."

I don't know if he's made up the answer, and I'm too lethargic to care.

"When will we get there?" I ask.

"Soon," he says. "It's just about five minutes." That's a family joke, a nod to the rubbery quality of Bhutanese time. It will be another five hours before we get to Trongsa, where we'll spend the night. The mere presence of a road in this rugged, mountainous terrain is a miracle. Mostly built by hand by the Bhutanese and the Indian Army, with Bhutanese, Indian, and Nepalese workers, the road is a marvelous engineering feat. Before the 1960s, there were only mule paths that crisscrossed the mountains. Consequently, it could take months to go from one end of the country to the other. Travelers had to use ropes to negotiate rivers where there were no bridges and face attack by wild animals and harsh weather, the two most harrowing dangers of travel here.

Namgay remembers when the road was being built near his village in Trongsa. He was about eight. He says some people ran away when the first vehicle, an Indian Mahindra Jeep, appeared—angry headlights flashing, horn blowing, to scare the life out of the villagers. In a country that's only about 200 miles wide as the crow flies, the lateral road, from Ha in the west to Chorten Kora in the east, covers about 300 miles as it winds around the sides of the mountains. Trongsa Dzong becomes an optical illusion, appearing close, then far away, then close again as the road zigzags. "Trongsa Dzong teases the people," Namgay says.

Sometimes the road is wide, about a lane and a half, and nicely paved. More often, it is pocked with potholes. Occasionally it narrows to a one-lane dirt track. Sometimes it all but disappears when landslides wash it away. The road is a lifeline, really. It belongs to everyone and everything: cars, trucks, buses, dogs, cows, people, bamboo, produce, and yak. If anything comes close to owning the road, it is the Tata trucks barreling, seemingly without mufflers, through the mountains carrying goods and sometimes people from one place to the other. Brightly painted with folk art, religious symbols, and anthropomorphic eyes above the headlights, their garish primary colors occasionally interrupted by dents, rust, and the odd missing piece, they look as if they came straight out of an American carnival in the 1950s. They carry impossibly large loads all over Bhutan, the goods covered in tarps and secured with hemp ropes that look as if they'll snap any second. Sometimes the loads are piled so high that the trucks become top-heavy and teeter alarmingly on the hairpin turns.

All the Tata truck drivers look like they're about

12 years old, their dark eyes alert and hardened and their arms thick and sinewy.

I recite part of "May," a John Clare poem I had to learn in the eighth grade, only I roll down the window so I can pound my hand on the side of the car, and I say it hip-hop style:

The driving boy beside his team

Of May-month beauty now will dream

And oft burst loud in fits of song

And whistle as he reels along

Cracking his whip in starts of joy

A happy dirty driving boy

I said a happy dirty driving boy

That's right a happy dirty driving boy

Dirty birdy driving boy

Namgay doesn't acknowledge my recitation. He's used to my odd behavior.

On the passenger side of every Tata ride boys even younger, assistants called *handi-boys*. They serve as an indispensable extra set of hands and eyes. When one of these elephantine trucks has to make a tight maneuver, the handi-boy pounds a drumbeat rhythm with his hand on the side or the back of the truck to guide the driver as he backs up or inches past another vehicle. *Thwack-THWACK! Thwack-THWACK! Thwack-THWACK!* When the pounding stops, the driver stops. The miracle is that these handi-boys, these princes of the road in whose hands we and the truck drivers place our lives and the well-being of those we carry, are often as young as eight.

Buses also have handi-boys. These "vomit comets" ply the roads with villagers inside and their bundles tied to the top. It costs less than $10 to go from one end of the country to the other. Expect no comfort on a long-distance bus ride in Bhutan. It is a tedious trip, taking five days, and if the bus breaks down or the road washes out, either or both of which you can pretty much count on, it will be much longer.

Every vehicle is packed to capacity with people and gear. People who have lived for many years in Thimphu still consider their villages home, so they go to see their relatives, to attend the annual family pujas, for births or deaths, for the census, or to vote. Often people have to park their cars and walk a few hours or a few days to get to their villages, since many people in Bhutan live in isolated hamlets far from the road.

In summer, impromptu vegetable and mushroom stands sprout up on either side of the road. These make convenient rest stops, a chance to get out and stretch your legs. There are very few restaurants, so you have to be sure to pack your own meals. Everyone has picnics at scenic spots. Of course, there aren't any toilets either. There is an unspoken rule that when we make a pit stop, boys go to the front of the vehicle and girls go to the back.

The road east out of Thimphu winds upward for about 45 minutes to Dochula Pass at 13,000 feet. Like all of the passes in Bhutan, Dochula is covered for several acres with multicolored prayer flags. It is auspicious to put prayer flags high up on the pass. The constant wind sends the prayers to heaven; the steady flapping of thousands of flags creates a satisfying snapping sound.

At the pass, Namgay takes off his baseball cap to

show respect for the mountain deities and says a short prayer. We pause to look at the view. If it's a clear day, which this one is, you can see the snowcapped Himalayas laid out for hundreds of miles. Gasa Dzong sits like a bright white bird far off on a mountain slope, and in the distance are the mountains of Tibet.

Ashi Dorji Wangmo Wangchuck, the eldest Queen Mother, has built 108 stupas on a knoll at the top of the pass. The scene looks like something the artist Christo would create if he converted to Tantric Buddhism. These white adobe structures stand about five feet tall, and their red-and-gold roofs glisten in the crystal-clear mountain air. With prayer flags draped over everything, they move me because she built them in honor of the fourth king, her husband, who in 2003 led the Bhutanese army in ousting several thousand Indian insurgents hiding in the jungles of southern Bhutan. Although the Indians were threatening Bhutan's sovereignty, the monument honors their fallen as well as the Bhutanese who lost their lives. Imagine having the wherewithal and the space and the resources of a country to build monuments to your husband, an enlightened monarch. It begs a comparison to Shah Jahan's creating one of the seven wonders of the world, the Taj Mahal, for his beloved wife. It's Biblical in scope, epic in its magnificent symbolism. *We're all living large in this tiny country,* I think.

A herd of goats is tailing some picnickers, two young men and two young girls, as they haul their baskets back to their car. The goats are begging for food like dogs. One of the men turns around and teases the largest one, a big white billy goat. He waves his jacket at him, and the short-tempered goat puts his head down and chases the man, giving him a short, sharp butt in the behind.

He could have done some damage, but this was just a warning to show who's the boss. Everyone laughs, including the man, but he quits teasing the goat.

On the other side of Dochula, we follow the road as it winds down through the forest and paddy to Punakha. In less than an hour the weather changes from brisk mountain air to semitropical: it's about 30 degrees hotter on the thermometer. Wearing layers is a good idea in Bhutan. As I struggle to take off my sweater in the car, we pass a mother washing her baby in a bucket on the side of the road.

High up above the pavement, in the outer reaches of the atmosphere, monasteries and temples dot the cliffs and mountainsides like fragile birds. I always spot one or two that I haven't noticed before, although I've traveled this road many times. They are hidden so far up in the mountains that a bend in the road, a half-second, can obscure a temple forever, as can a shadow or a cloud.

We come to the prayer wheel built over a mountain stream at the side of the road. People often stop here to wash their cars, so we call it the Bhutanese Car Wash. Our car is clean, so we keep going down the mountain.

The orange trees, poinsettia bushes, and acres of rice paddies begin terracing the hills. The walls of farmhouses halfway up the mountainsides shine white in the sunlight. On the left, just at the turnoff to Punakha, Chimi Lhakhang, the temple built by Drukpa Kunley, sits on a knoll. It is said that if a woman takes the blessing at Chimi Lhakhang, which includes being anointed on the head with a large wooden phallus, she will have a child. Past Punakha, just before we cross the bridge and switchback up the mountain to Wangdue, we stop at the Dragon's Nest Hotel Restaurant for lunch. Namgay eats two plates of noodles slathered in hot sauce. I don't like this particular brand of Indian hot sauce or this leg of the trip. I'm feeling peevish because a few miles back I realized I'd forgotten my hiking boots.

I drink an orange soda, and he tells me I should eat more, not just drink a nuclear-colored cola loaded with sugar. I don't feel like eating, the sugar has kicked in, and so I tell him to piss off. It's not like I have one every day, or every month even. Having to get out of the car and sit in the restaurant, which is empty except for us, and be at the mercy of a wait staff that clearly wishes we were not there, has magnified my bad mood. Besides, riding in the car is tiring, but Namgay wants to keep driving.

We get back into the car and sit stoically next to each other. We do not speak for several miles. Then he starts laughing. "We're *saagays*," he says. *Idiots*.

"Why?" I ask.

"We fight for no reason."

"I'm sorry," I say, and we are happy again.

In Wangdue town, the hotels, bars, and shops hug the road as it doglegs around the ridgeline. Built at odd angles, they all look like they are about to fall down. The only thing substantial on them is the fresh coat of whitewash and the Bhutanese painting that covers everything. The buildings are so close to the road that, if you're not careful, you could wind up in someone's living room. As it is, you can see customers chatting together, eating, and drinking inside the dimly lit hotel restaurants. They are like little tableaus as we drive slowly past.

A new Wangdue town is built below the old one. It has more room and easier access to Punakha town. It's also closer to the river. The town center of Punakha, too, has already been relocated to an area that is larger and flatter and has room to grow.

After Wangdue, the road becomes more treacherous as it winds around the mountains toward Trongsa. This section belongs to large monkey troops, cows, and road workers whose rattan huts are constructed inches from the road and sometimes on it. We stop the car and watch a mother monkey and her baby warily eyeing us. Then they run off into the trees.

We pass a short stretch of road—about 50 feet—that has dropped into the ravine below. The Indian Army is contracted to keep the roads of Bhutan in working order, so they import Indian and Nepali workers. These lost souls with shredded clothing and blank stares have dug a narrow corridor under a ledge to act as a temporary thoroughfare until they can put a Bailey bridge, a structure made of prefab metal parts meant to fix a road fast, over the hole.

I instinctively lift my feet up and hold my breath as Namgay maneuvers the car through the slippery mud. His side of the car almost scrapes the cliff wall. I can't stop myself from looking left. On my side of the car is the abyss, and I think about death. I can only see the tops of trees about 500 feet below us.

After we pass, Namgay stops and has a word with the supervisor. They speak together in Nepali, and it sounds very somber. Heavy rains made this fissure in the earth two days before. A family—mother, father, and two children in a Maruti van—had the bad karma to be driving on just this spot when the landslide hit. They were swept down into the gorge, their vehicle buried. It had to be excavated from the mud by road workers. I shudder.

Landslides are frequent in the rainy season. People often walk around the debris and trade vehicles with people going in the other direction. Once there was a particularly nasty mudslide near Phuentsholing that cut a giant V shape about 30 feet into the earth and tore away the road. When we arrived on the scene, people in a long line of cars were waiting to slide down the near side of the V, one by one, to reach the bottom, where a big yellow Caterpillar tractor maneuvered itself behind each car and pushed it up the other side.

Just past the landslide, we come to a detour to Gangtey, a medieval-looking town built on the side of a hill, with a crooked little road and houses on either side. At the top of the hill, Gangtey Dzong commands a spectacular view of the wide, achingly beautiful valley of Phobjikha that spreads out for miles. Here we deliver a package to some monk, a relative of Namgay's, then continue to Pelela Pass. Here the road meanders down through rich farmland and hardwood forests. This is Trongsa and the Black Mountains, the heart of Bhutan. Yak graze here in the winter; but it is not yet cold enough, so the herds are higher up in the alpine pastures. Around Trongsa, farmers lay big trunks of bamboo on the road for cars and trucks to run over. It's an efficient way to split the cane so it can be woven into mats and baskets.

Chendebji Chorten is about halfway to Trongsa town. It is down in a little gorge on the side of the road, and within the last few years numerous other chortens and stupas have been built nearby.

"Are we stopping here?" I ask when we reach the chorten.

"Compulsory," says Namgay.

I laugh.

He stops the car, and we get out. I bring out a big thermos, two cups, and some biscuits, and we sit on a mat in the grass to enjoy the tea and sunshine and watch the spectacle of the road.

Namgay calls my attention to a bird singing nearby. He says its name is *lhab bya* (lab by-ya) and he remembers it from his childhood.

"When we hear that bird call, it's a sad time," he says.

"Why sad?"

"Because all of last year's rice is gone and the new rice we just planted hasn't come yet. We're hungry."

When the bird sings again, I realize it is a nightingale. It would have migrated from its winter nesting grounds in early spring. As a child, Namgay, lying in bed with an empty stomach, would have heard the bird singing all night. A wave of sadness hits me. There is so much in the world I can't do anything about. I vow to be nicer.

When we get to the Jakar valley and Bumthang, it's midday and we go straight to Jambey Lhakhang, the ancient temple where our family's puja is to take place. There are about 30 relatives and friends already gathered there in festive party mode. There's plenty of laughter and joking, but everyone is busy—hauling water, cutting vegetables, and unpacking food. They appear to be expecting an army and are ready to feed hundreds of people for three days.

Namgay's relatives are civil servants from Thimphu and village people who live below the mountain in the village of Chendebji. Some are from the neighboring villages, and their lives are crowded with work from sunup to sundown. The puja is a welcome break from their labors. But the Bhutanese from Namgay's village don't discriminate as we Westerners do between what is play and what is work. They often play as hard as they work, as they are doing now. Even though it is a break from their routine, they are hard at it, making preparations.

Some of the men are standing outside the kitchen passing around a big skin full of ara. Other workers and volunteers are unloading and organizing large baskets and gunnysacks of food. The kitchen, in the field behind the *lhakhang* (temple), is a long, low mud building with a tin roof. The large mud stove in the corner already has several sizeable pots boiling on it. There is an open fire in the middle of the kitchen. An old man sits beside it and sharpens a big *kichu* knife to carve the meat.

There are more than 700 pounds of rice stacked in burlap bags under the windows. There are also 90 pounds of chicken, 150 pounds of beef, 90 pounds of cheese for making ema datse, 6 pounds of tea, 18 pounds of sugar, 20 pounds of milk powder, and 90 pounds of vegetables. The nearby stacks of beef—cows' legs and ribs and various body parts that will be cut up by the old man sharpening the knife—look out of place in such a holy Buddhist setting. Buddhism is about the sanctity of all life, but many Bhutanese aren't vegetarian. They like to eat meat. I think, like so many things in Bhutan, it's about survival. Meat is good protein. It is a paradox, but traditional, to give the monks plenty of meat since they are the most important element of the puja. Without them there is no ceremony. They get breakfast, a midmorning tea break, lunch, a midafternoon tea break, and dinner. As I sit outside in the warm sun, I hear them chanting, and then there is the unmistakable sound of a conch shell being blown.

When the conch shell is blown in rituals, it represents the Buddha's teachings, which spread in all directions. When you hear the sound of the conch, you are being asked to wake up. The conch shell is one of the Eight Auspicious Symbols. There's a set of these signs decorating a wall in the courtyard of the temple. They are stacked on top of each other, going up the side of a column. I love the way the iconography instructs the people in Bhutan, explicitly or intuitively. It satisfies the teacher in me, as well as the student.

There are at least 108 monks to perform the ceremony, 108 being an auspicious number. But the count is never exact, because some monks bring their friends. Along with the three buses of monks we brought from Trongsa Dzong and a monastery in Bumthang, we have to be ready to feed anybody else who shows up.

Bumthang was the home of Terton Pema Lingpa, the treasure finder who lived about six centuries ago. It's where I met the schoolchildren and the pink goat almost ten years ago. Now I am with my Bhutanese family; and we are having this ceremony in one of the oldest and most beautiful temples in the country, as well as the holiest. To honor the deities in the holiest temple in Bhutan is fortunate for our family. We are prosperous and healthy. We give thanks.

The walls of the several altar rooms are black with the smoke of 1,000 years of incense and butter lamps. Faint images, painted centuries ago, are just visible in the candlelight. It isn't the opulence of the place that makes it so special—although the statues, prayer books, and ritual objects in it must be priceless—it is the palpable emotional and spiritual well-being it gives all of us. Outside, two old women are doing prostrations.

The next morning we wake before dawn and go to the lhakhang. We dressed in ghos and kiras and carry ceremonial scarves. I have no official duties, so I can simply sit in the temple with the monks and listen and meditate. Namgay spends most of his time cooking and organizing the serving of the food. In addition to the monks, 60 elderly Bhutanese come to the temple daily to pray and socialize. This happens in every temple in Bhutan; it's a sort of senior daycare. The old people pray for their families and for the monks. They say, *"Om mane padme hung,"* the prayer to Chenrezig, the Compassion Buddha. He is the one who will help them move to their next lives when they die.

We will feed all of these old people, the monks, our family, pilgrims to the lhakhang, and whoever else wanders into the area. Luckily, most village people in Bhutan carry their dishes with them inside their hemchus, the pockets of their ghos and kiras. It's an old tradition.

The puja is an expression of our faith and our hope for the future. We are paying our respects to the deities and asking for continued blessings in return. Watching the puja unfold is an interesting reflection of the resilience and creativity of my Bhutanese family and their friends. With so few resources the Bhutanese are able to pull off minor miracles. They toil and struggle with grace and with so much dignity. Wealth in Bhutan doesn't come from money.

In intervals during the three days of the puja, I daydream as the monks chant, blow horns, and beat drums. Then I sit in the sun or walk around the outside of the temple with the elderly people. With my broken Dzongkha I talk to them a little, and they crowd around me to get a word in. I am a novelty.

"Your Dzongkha is very good!" one old woman says, stretching the truth.

I smile. "My Dzongkha is not good," I respond.

"You're so fat!" another old woman says as she gets a good grip on my upper arm, zeroing in on the place where I feel most vulnerable and, well, fat. But this conversation has no room for my vanity. I know what to say.

"Do you really mean it, or are you just trying to flatter me?" I ask. Saying someone is fat isn't an insult in the villages of Bhutan; it's a compliment. *Fat* doesn't mean fat so much as it means healthy and prosperous.

"No flattery," she says. "I mean it! You're really fat!"

"Thank you, thank you, thank you," I say. "You're fat, too."

She smiles shyly. I've made her day.

Toward the end of the liturgy, which is a series of invocations to local deities, Guru Rinpoche, the Compassion Buddha, and others—even wrathful deities in the Buddhist pantheon—the monks and lamas begin perambulating around the central altar of the main temple. As they stand up, I also stand. One high lama motions for me to slip into the procession behind him. We pass the front of the ancient altar with 1,000 butter lamps flickering on a large wooden table and make our way to a narrow passage beside the main altar that I've never noticed before. There is an overpowering smell of cedar incense, and torpid smoke languishes at waist level.

A dark walkway leads behind the altar. The slit windows in the ancient passageway give only enough light to show shadows of the monks' feet. I feel as though I am being carried along on their flowing red robes. The stone floor is cold and uneven under my bare feet. As my eyes adjust to the darkness, I catch a glimpse of Namgay and one of his cousins ahead of me, surrounded by the monk procession. I realize the whole family must be here.

We walk the auspicious 108 times around the central altar in an ancient purification ritual while the monks chant prayers for our well-being. Their voices vibrate off the stone walls. Afterward, we go outside. Everyone is looking up, shading their eyes. There is a rainbow around the sun.

Heading home after the puja, we get a late start to Trongsa. We are driving up the Yotongla Pass in the dark, with dense gray fog all around. We can see only a few inches in front of the car on the narrow, winding mountain road. Not many people drive these roads after dark, and certainly not in fog. Just before the fog started rolling down the mountain, we were talking about yet another recent accident on this very same road. A school bus plunged over the side, killing a doctor and severely injuring other passengers. Death is never far away in Bhutan. Below the pass, potholes make us go slow. But on the other side of Trongsa, in the valley, the fog gives way to a luminous black night. We can see Chendebji Chorten shining white in the distance. Specters of other stupas and prayer flags surrounding it appear out of the mist.

We stop at the house of a cousin of Namgay's, where we will stay for the night. I sit in her kitchen sipping tea in front of the woodstove. I can see the stars through the cracks in her kitchen wall, as it is made of cane matting. A generator gives the barest hint of light from a solitary bulb. It makes everything look sepia-soft and dreamlike.

The cousin, Yeshe, is busy cooking a chicken. In the next room, three forestry guards sit at the end of a large table sipping whiskey. They talk and laugh, and occasionally one of them turns to sneak a look at me. It is a little unusual to have a foreigner in the kitchen. The house is the only place for miles around with electricity, so it is a popular meeting spot. I try to act Bhutanese by sitting quietly and not moving much. By not drawing attention to myself, I am showing respect. This is their place to relax.

Namgay goes down to the river to set up our tent. After a meal, we go to sleep enveloped by darkness and the sounds of forest life—birds calling and a lonely dog barking. Namgay says dogs bark at night because they see things in the shadows, ghosts or spirits. When we visit the U.S., he doesn't sleep well, because, he says, the lack of dogs barking keeps him awake.

The next morning is mercifully bright and sunny, as we want to go to a family temple about three hours' walk above the village. The temple has recently been painted and refurbished, so there is a consecration ceremony. Yeshe has a pair of boots that fit me. The trail goes straight up the mountain through a dense forest dotted with sandstone caves. On the way there, we see tiger tracks.

We keep walking straight up into the clouds. Behind us are the Black Mountains, a dense and foreboding hardwood forest that comprises half of Trongsa and part of Zhemgang District. It is a national forest and a protected area. There are surely tigers there. Bengal tigers are migrating to Bhutan from West Bengal in India, where they are hunted and their habitats are disappearing. The tigers have never lived above 3,000 feet, but now they do. They're adapting.

"Look there. Tigers are always living there," Namgay says, pointing to a cave. I think of the *thanka* he has just painted. Part of it shows a mountain sliced open to reveal the labyrinth of tiger caves inside it.

We walk up to a high mountain meadow where Namgay used to bring the family's cows and sheep to graze.

"When you were a boy did you ever think you'd be bringing your American wife here?"

"No," he says.

"Isn't it strange?"

"It's our life," he says, unwilling to make a judgment. I let his words resonate in my mind. I love his equanimity and self-control, the things I lack. We are yin and yang.

We reach the top of the mountain, which is bald except for enormous bamboo gardens, some of them half an acre in diameter. They are surrounded by bamboo-cane fencing and have been cultivated for centuries. The tall bamboo trees rustle in the breeze. The small temple sits in the middle of this bamboo forest at the top of the mountain. From the distance, we can hear the horns and drums of the consecration puja, in progress since the early morning.

We've brought a few things in our packs, but the rest of the meat, biscuits, and treats from Thimphu are coming a little later, around lunchtime, on the backs of horses. There is a large gate and a courtyard in the temple. Namgay's aunt is the caretaker of the temple and lives here with her husband. She's planted mustard greens that are fed by a little spring on the side of the yard. A water-driven prayer wheel turns clockwise. It has a little bell attached to it that goes *ting ting ting* as the wheel spins and the bell hits a nail in the wooden bracket that holds the wheel in place.

The temple is modest, but the recent refurbishing has been a massive undertaking. It had to be done, as the temple was over 300 years old and badly in need of repair. The wood had rotted and the mud walls had cracked. So everything was removed: the canvas thanka paintings on the walls were painstakingly peeled off and rolled up, the walls knocked down, the wood replaced, and then the walls rebuilt with pounded mud. The ancient paintings were then glued onto the new walls.

I have seen other temples being restored. Village women stand up on top of the walls, using hoe-like implements to pound the mud. They sing songs while they're doing it to help them keep the rhythm and to pass the time.

There are nine monks and a lama in the main temple room. The lamas sit opposite the choshom, an altar with statues, flowers, incense, and butter lamps. There are also tall, colorful tormas, the most elaborate I think I've ever seen. It takes several people working all day to make the dough and color it, then shape the sculptures. Someone at this temple worked very hard. Below the altar is a bench full of offerings of *cabze* cakes, fruit, rice, and sweets. The puja is done to appease the local deities, to thank them for a good life and to encourage them to look favorably on all of our households.

I sit down on a rug near the door, fish in my pocket for a mint, and pull out a piece of paper I've made some notes on:

> Use the word farther *to designate physical distance, as in: we went farther into the woods than we have ever gone.* Further *indicates advancement along a nonphysical dimension: we can't decide where to go until we're further along in the research.*

The farther I go into Bhutan, the further I get in understanding my own ideas and motivations. Sometimes we have to go the physical distance, to struggle with real mountains, to help bring us further along on our mental or spiritual journey. I suppose that's the reason for pilgrimages.

I look up, and the lama in the center of the room motions for me to come to him. I get up and stand in front of him; he motions for me to bend down. He takes a white silk scarf and drapes it around my neck as he says a prayer. Then he knocks me on the crown of my head with his knuckle. It feels playful. I look up. He grins. Is it part of the ceremony? I don't know, but I am awash in goodwill from the thump on the head by this lama. I feel like he is letting me in on some joke, or maybe it's a warning. Either way, he's making me feel a part of the day. I decide it is both.

Namgay appears in the doorway. I bow to the lama and turn and walk over to Namgay.

"I'm so happy to be here. Thank you," I say.

"For what?"

"For everything."

He looks at me and smiles, but doesn't say anything.

Decay is inherent in all compounded things.
Work out your salvation with diligence.

— BUDDHA'S LAST WORDS

As Long as We Both Shall Live

During summer monsoons the weather becomes a preoccupation in Bhutan. In this area near the Indian Ocean, heavy rains dominate our lives for about three months.

During this time, you can forget about being dry. Everything—trees, dirt, clothing, food, books, beds—swells with wetness. Throw a moist shirt in the corner and in a few hours it sprouts little black spots of mildew that never wash out. Showering is redundant. Walking in town in the afternoon feels lumberous, like swimming upstream. Everything is green, puffed-up, animated, and ripe.

It's not just the wet we have to deal with. Sometimes we have shortages because the roads wash out. Four years ago Thimphu ran out of food—no oil, no milk, no eggs, and we were low on rice—during a particularly rainy August.

Monsoon means "season" in Arabic and has to do with wind that changes direction. Geologists believe that 20 million years ago this ancient weather pattern slammed the Indian subcontinent into the rest of Asia, creating the Himalayas and the Tibetan Plateau. And apparently India is still pushing; it makes the mountains an inch taller each year.

During monsoons, gray clouds curl violently over the mountains, crash into cliffs, pour into valleys, and spill tank-sized loads of rain. The season lasts from about mid-June to mid-September.

In the monsoon this year, the rain was slow to start but came relentlessly. It washed away the road to Phuentsholing in minutes, tearing away the earth and leaving big, black, yawning holes and gushing water-falls down the mountainsides.

Everybody expects natural disasters at this time, and they're ready for them: Bhutanese and Indian soldiers erect Bailey bridges in the big open spaces where roads used to hug the sides of cliffs. When all of the three roads into the country are washed away for several miles by the monsoon, Bhutan is locked up tight.

Druk Air has two Airbus planes that fly into Bhutan. They must make one of the most harrowing landings in the world, into Paro Airport, which is situated in a short, high, narrow valley. The only airport higher than Paro is the one at La Paz, Bolivia, but that's on a big plateau and can accommodate a wide-body jet. A plane can't fly into Paro using instruments; the pilot has to be able to see the runway to land. Flights can't land in cloudy weather or in the dark. If it's hot or inclement weather and the plane needs more speed, more fuel, or less weight, the crew will leave some or all of the baggage behind in Calcutta. So you might get to Paro, but your clothes and toothbrush may stay in India. During the monsoon there is a low, gray-white ceiling over the mountains that makes us feel like we're in a big white dome. We know that no planes will come for days.

Even as Bhutan evolves and modernizes, it is as if the geography and weather are holding it back. Nature is saying, "Not so fast." But the Bhutanese are philosophical about it. They take things as they come.

I think it has something to do with the fact that they see things in a continuum. They don't have to have everything in this lifetime. They have an ease with death and dying, maybe because the end isn't the end if you believe in reincarnation. It's just a blip on the screen of your existence, a momentary setback, an intermission in the movie—go out and get some popcorn and it will all start again. A friend of Namgay's, a young monk in his 20s, has been in poor health his whole life. He has rheumatoid arthritis and probably a few other chronic illnesses, and one day he told Namgay that he was ready to die and reincarnate. He wanted to roll the cosmic dice and get himself a new body.

When people die in Bhutan, being good Buddhists, they are cremated. In summer, the time between a death and a cremation is very short. Some Bhutanese have been known to do a makeshift embalming with salt if the body can't be cremated for a while, but mostly the Bhutanese are concerned not so much with the dead body as with the spirit of the dead loved one. Cremation is to help the spirit find its way to its next reincarnation. It is said that some high holy men didn't smell when they died—sometimes, in fact, they even

gave off a nice perfume. These men were cremated after 48 days of ceremony.

A Bhutanese friend of mine who runs a tour company had an odd British trekking client. The client came alone in February without a coat, though there was still plenty of snow in the mountains where he was heading. His guide, his cook, and the other staff on the trek tried to dissuade him from going, but he wouldn't listen. They loaned him a coat.

Some people come to Bhutan to die because they think it is an auspicious place to achieve their next life. Or they want to die far from the prying eyes of their loved ones. This strange, lonely tourist succeeded. He had a heart attack and died in his sleep in a tent halfway to Jumolarhi, the sacred mountain. The tour company hired soldiers to bring the body down from the mountains over narrow, rocky trails. It was a four-day walk down to the town of Paro from the side of the remote mountain where he gave up the ghost.

The soldiers put the deceased in an empty tour bus, parked it in a paddy outside of Paro, and waited for word from his family in England about what to do with his remains. Even in February, the Himalayan sun was very hot at midday, and the body simmered and swelled in the metal bus. The smell became unbearable. There were no facilities at the hospital or anywhere else to keep a corpse. There was no morgue. A pack of dogs intermittently ran in a mad circle around the bus, then stopped still and wailed.

I heard my friend on the telephone pleading to some official in England, "The lamas say tomorrow is a very auspicious day. If we could cremate him then, it would be good." The day probably was auspicious, but the real reason for the urgency was that the poor man was becoming a health hazard. My friend was too polite and Bhutanese to say that, though. This went on for two days before she got permission from a relative in Wales to cremate the body.

Tibetans sometimes practice sky burial for their dead. They take the bodies to a high, holy place and hack them into pieces to be food for vultures. It is a last act of compassion, completely selfless, to feed other sentient beings with one's own remains, and it is thought to help one have a better reincarnation. Sky burial is not common in Bhutan. A Bhutanese friend says that his entire life, he's known only one man who had sky burial because he requested it. Still, urban legend Bhutanese-style says that in the past the practice was popular, and it's said that once a baby's arm fell from the sky onto the street in downtown Thimphu.

The Bhutanese are more comfortable with death than Americans, and Buddhism teaches that we should think of death at least five times every day. We in the U.S. are less likely to think about death, even when we see it in the movies, because what we see of it is not really death. We get our death simulated, or pumped with embalming fluid, dressed up, and laid out for viewing. It's on television or YouTube. As a result, we're not on very good terms with death. This is understandable—it's about our fear of the unknown—but the experience of death is exactly the opposite in Bhutan. It is embraced as a natural function, a positive step, a way to move on to the next life, a chance to spin the big karmic wheel. And you're more likely to run into death "in the flesh" in Bhutan.

The monsoons and all this water make me think of life and death. The river flows through Thimphu before it runs beside our house. It starts from some ancient glacier that melts in the High Himalayas and makes its way through the narrow river valleys of Laya and Gasa. The Thimphu valley is a little less narrow. There are horse trails and orchards and vast forests covering much of the high, steep mountains above the town. Many ancient monasteries and temples sit aloof above it all, amid prayer flags and stupas. They take many hours to reach on foot; some take days and are perched, impossibly, on cliffs. If you know where to look, you can see the sunlight play on their golden roofs.

This is where the real action is in Bhutan. There, among the prayer flags and clouds and chortens and steaming hot springs, an army, thousands strong, of Buddhist monks and nuns prays and performs rituals to sway the world to sanity, peace, and enlightenment. There's real magic in the mountains, up close to the spirits. I often think they are controlling our lives down below, making things happen or not happen, like Zeus and Hera and the other Greek gods and goddesses. It is a realm between the earth and sky, a demi-heaven, where mortality is secondary to transcendence.

Namgay was identified at about age seven as potential monk material and sent to study with a relative, a high Buddhist lama. For three years he lived with the lama in the village. Then he went to Kuertoe, in Lhuntse in far eastern Bhutan, with an uncle, another lama, where he endured a Dickens-like existence caring for the holy man, making his food, washing his clothes, walking about the country assisting in religious ceremonies, learning to read and interpret religious texts, and planting and growing vegetables. He lived there for three years as well. He had no shoes or shirt. He missed his family. It was a difficult time for him.

When this uncle was young, he had worked in the dzong in Wangdue as an assistant to the thrimpon at the high court. He had a baby daughter and a wife who lived in the town. But one day the uncle vanished. Namgay's mother and grandmother went to Thimphu to report the disappearance to the police. But the police couldn't help. He had disappeared and left no trace.

Twenty-three years passed. One day, Namgay's father was in Trongsa market with a cow he wanted to sell. A *Kuertop*, a man from the area around Kuertoe, came by and bought the cow. After the sale, over a celebratory glass of ara, they started talking, as people do, about their families and where they lived.

"What about your wife's family? Where are they from?" asked the Kuertop. "Rugubjche," said Namgay's father. "One brother is a farmer, one is a monk, and one disappeared."

How they figured the next bit out Namgay isn't sure, but the Kuertop said that Namgay's uncle, the one who had disappeared, had been living in Kuertoe as a hermit for over 20 years. He was now a lama. So Namgay's father and his uncle the farmer went to Kuertoe and found the runaway brother. He'd spent all those years in meditation in India and Sikkim and Bhutan. If it seems strange that he abandoned his family for the spiritual life, there was a precedent: the Buddha renounced all of his worldly possessions, his palace, and his birthright as a prince; he left his mother, father, young wife, and baby boy to seek the answer to why we suffer and, eventually, to seek and achieve enlightenment.

Uncle Lama comes to our house sometimes when he's in Thimphu. He's very old now and nothing but bones, and he hardly speaks. Namgay remembers that when they left Trongsa to live in Kuertoe, his uncle was middle-aged and plump.

I think this man will have no problem when he dies. The Bhutanese say that when people die, if they haven't meditated, then they often get confused. Some of them don't know they're dead. They sit with the family at meals and get mad because they're snubbed and not offered food. But if they've meditated, then they know which road to take when they die. They don't hang around at the family dinner hour, but go straight on to their next rebirth—or, if they're lucky, they finish the cycle and go to Nirvana.

I've read that Tantric masters can alter their physical bodies, attain a "subtle body," and learn to operate on an astral plane, or a light plane. This physical manipulation through meditation and yoga is Kundalini from India, or something related to it, that predates Buddhism. These masters can control their blood and semen, semen being the life force. This is what gives them their transcending power.

"Can your uncle control his *taku*?" I ask Namgay.

"Why would my uncle want to control his walnuts?" he asks, laughing. And being evasive. The word for walnut is *tako* in Dzongkha. Semen is *taku*. He knows I can't keep them straight.

Although he laughs, this is serious business. Namgay believes we must respect the secret nature of the ritual. It's not something to be idly chatted about. And he knows, firsthand, that knowledge of sacred rituals will change a person. There is no going back. Still, I try to imagine what it must look like: Tantric masters sitting in caves, on rocks, on thrones like big lamas in temples, wearing robes or cloaks made from silks or animal skins, or wearing loin cloths, or naked and painted like a sadhu, a Hindu mystic.

These masters have many talents. Some, if they are really advanced, can turn themselves into birds or other animals. They can fly. They can separate the self, the body, and the soul. Good practice for death, I suppose.

On a walk one afternoon to a temple above our house, I am trying to absorb this idea.

"When he flies, how does he do it?" I ask Namgay.

"Who?"

"Your uncle. Like a bird? Does he flap his arms?"

"Not like that," Namgay says dismissively.

We get to the temple, and the caretaker comes out and starts to talk to Namgay in *Mongpa*, their local language, so I drop the subject.

Later that evening, when he's in the kitchen chopping onions for dinner, I go in and start making the rice.

"How does he do it?" I don't want to let it rest.

"Not like a bird," he says, slicing an onion. "More like a helicopter." He smiles, evasive to the end.

"Did you ever see him fly?" I ask.

"No," he says gravely. "That would be bad."

"Why bad?"

He lowers his eyes and slices a big chunk of onion. "It's not for me to see that he flies."

This cryptic answer ends the conversation. What can I say? I know when I'm licked.

There is much I will never understand. I have learned that asking questions, trying to find the underlying cause of things, is most often futile. Of course, I routinely pursue the unpursuable, but I have also learned that if I stop a line of inquiry and observe, and if I'm quiet and don't ask the question, the answer occasionally comes. Maybe I have to wait. Maybe it's not the answer I anticipated. The answer is in the skill of asking—that is, it's not asking questions that matters so much, but it is about asking what is skillful.

This is a hard lesson for Westerners. We are locked into a very narrow way of thinking. Descartes really screwed us over. "I think, therefore I am" means that a lot of things are actually beyond us if our being is dependent on our comprehension. It's good to be rational, but a little spontaneity is also beneficial, as is an occasional grand leap of faith.

When I was young and impressionable, I was fortunate enough to read a great book called *My Name Is Aram* by William Saroyan. The title character has an uncle who is full of tall tales. At the end of the book Aram questions the uncle, doubting some of his stories. The uncle says, "Believe in everything." They are the last words of the book, the punch line, the payoff, the raison d'être. It's fantastic advice, especially if you move to a place where there's magic.

Every morning during the monsoons, when it's not raining and sometimes when it is, Namgay and I go outside and drink coffee. We spend a lot of time standing or sitting in the yard or leaning on the stone wall looking at the river, especially near dawn and sunset. Eagle-eyed Namgay, raised in the forests of the Himalayas, can spot Coke bottles and all manner of flotsam as it hurries by. As the days progress, we marvel at how high the river gets, swelling over its banks, coming nearer and nearer to rocks and trees, which have become our markers, eventually to consume them. It's infinitely entertaining. We call it River TV.

One afternoon Namgay called my attention to what looked like a bunch of clothes caught on a rock. But it wasn't just a bunch of clothes. Or was it? At first, we thought it was a doll. But there seemed to be a tiny body. It seemed to be lashed by its clothing to a rock in the middle of the river. It was mostly under the water, just below the surface, but if you studied it, you could see its hands, its nose, as it swirled and they pierced the glassy surface for just a second, until they disappeared in the white water.

I was stunned. It really looked like a corpse. It had long black hair—a girl. My spontaneous thought was that if the child were alive, she would certainly enjoy swirling and twirling in the river like that. She would be laughing.

"I've never seen anything like that," I cried.

"Sometimes when babies die people put them in the river," Namgay said calmly, leaning against the stone wall.

"But why? Why don't they cremate them?" I tried to look away. Caught in the universal dilemma of rubberneckers everywhere, I couldn't stop watching her twisting ghoulishly in the river.

"They don't if the child is young. They put it in the river," he said.

Cremation is expensive. There are all kinds of rituals involved, and rituals mean you have to feed a lot of people and pay a lot of monks. And it can go on for days, weeks, months, even years.

We went inside. Later, I went back and stood there beside the river until it got so dark I couldn't see her anymore.

Namgay had been inside for some time. I wanted to

go in, too, but I felt guilty leaving, so I stayed for a while, trying to think. He was in the kitchen finishing a sandwich when I finally came in, his appetite undeterred.

"What are we going to do?" I asked. I was in full-on American mode: alert the authorities; call the police; spring into action; clean this mess up; call the undertaker.

"It will rain tonight, and the river will carry it away," he said, spreading butter on another piece of bread.

"We have to call the police."

"No. Then so many problems."

"What problems?"

"The family will be disturbed unnecessarily."

"It's a dead baby."

"It got sick and died."

"Maybe the baby wasn't sick. Maybe they killed it, then dumped it in the river." I hadn't spent the early part of my life watching cop shows for nothing.

"No," he said. "Bhutanese people don't do like this."

I had to agree. The Bhutanese, generally speaking, adored their children and took very good care of them. They spoiled them, really. Mothers nursed their babies for years, and the babies' feet hardly touched the ground the first few years of their lives.

I went back outside to look. She was still there in the river. I felt horrible.

Back inside, Namgay was making dinner. He stood at the kitchen sink, pouring rice into the green plastic tub we use to wash food. I stood nearby, wondering what to do. I happened to notice the burlap bag of rice sitting next to the sink. It was from India. The label said: "Basmati Rice—Nurtured by Himalayan Waters."

I let out a loud cackle and pointed to the bag. "That baby will help the rice grow," I said, hearing the hysteria in my voice. He looked at the bag, then turned around and lit the stove to make a pot of tea. He told me to go sit down, that he would finish making dinner.

I sat at the dining-room table. After a few minutes, he brought me tea.

All night I couldn't sleep. The dead baby was next to us, asleep in the river; and worst of all, I could hear water flowing. Every night we were lulled to sleep by its sweet sound, the endless loop of white noise; but now, this night, the noise was taunting me. I felt exhausted but wired. My mind was racing. *How did she die? Why did she get stuck to the rock, our rock, in the river right next to our house? Were the cosmos trying to tell me something? Would she be there in the morning?* It's too sad when a baby dies. It felt like I was mourning.

Old habits being what they are, it was still distressing to me to live in a part of the world where death and decay were all around me, were so accepted, so much a part of daily living. As an American, I'd be happy to kick the bucket, pop my clogs, meet my maker, fall off my perch, pass away, pass on, expire like a can of potted meat (or, as they say here, pass my sell-by date), pack it in, pack it up, breathe my last breath, go to my reward, go to meet Jesus, bite the dust, or give up the ghost. I just don't want to *die*. Or look at a dead baby spinning in the river beside my house.

Namgay said again that a good rain would swell the river and the corpse would pass, perhaps go all the way down to India and join the Brahmaputra as it makes its way to Bangladesh and meets the Ganges. It could go all the way to Varanasi. "All Indian rivers originate in Bhutan," he said. I wasn't sure about that, but I didn't want to argue.

I couldn't wait for the corpse to be dislodged. I suggested that we get one of the Indian workers who were building a house across the river to go and cut it loose. Every day for lunch the workers went down to the river, stripped down to their loincloth rags, and washed and relaxed and played and lounged around. Maybe they'd even noticed the baby.

Namgay said no, that we should give it more time, and anyway, how would anyone make it across this river? No one could swim in the powerful current.

I was miserable. Damn, where was a flying lama when you needed him?

On farms in Tennessee, if a dog kills a chicken once, then it is likely to do it again. It gets a taste for poultry. A farm dog is no good if it kills chickens; so to break the dog of the habit, a farmer ties a dead chicken around the dog's neck. The animal has to go around with the putrid corpse tied to it for days. Dogs are generally pretty comfortable with decaying things, but for some reason this is absolute torture for a dog, and it will quit killing chickens. I felt tortured with the baby floating in the river beside our house. But I couldn't complete the analogy.

I was fascinated by my angst and Namgay's lack of angst. He hardly reacted at all. This was an Asian thing, specifically a Buddhist thing, to have this ease with death. I worried about decay, the baby's and my own; and that was, I guess, the reason I wanted it gone. In less than a day, it had taken over my life.

The night before, I had said, "Maybe it's bad karma to have the baby there in the river next to the house. Maybe our luck will go down." This is a phrase he uses all the time. He is preoccupied with luck or lack of it.

"No bad karma," he said, and turned over in bed.

"What about the ghost?" I persisted. "It's probably still around." He usually worries about ghosts, too, especially if he's gone to the cremation ground. He always has a little ceremony, a purging of ghosts, with incense and chanting on the doorstep before he'll enter the house after a cremation.

"The ghost is nowhere near here," he said definitively.

Rats. "What about the naga?" I persisted. "Maybe they won't like it. They don't like much of anything."

"The naga don't care," he said. Then gently, "Sleep."

But I couldn't.

My worry over something not alive vexed him as much as the baby troubled me. The baby's soul was long out of this life, by his reckoning, and well on its way to the next. It was just what happened sometimes, he said, when a human being's life had been cut off prematurely in a previous life. "Sometimes they come back and they live for a year or two, then they die. They're just finishing out the samsara."

This explanation was not consoling.

So we lived with the corpse in the river for another day.

That night, I went to bed early. Namgay was painting, and I could hear his soft chanting. In the middle of the night, I woke with a start. I'd dreamed a raven called from a tree beside the house. In the dream, I looked and Namgay wasn't beside me in bed. I went downstairs. He wasn't in the kitchen either. I walked through the house, then opened the door and went outside. The raven was still calling, *caw, caw, caw.*

It wasn't raining, but there had been a heavy rain, so everything was alive with wet, and water dripped from the eaves of the house and the trees. The sky was full of broken clouds; and a full moon peeked through, making everything bright and luminous, but with strange shadows. My own arms and legs, sticking out of my nightgown, seemed to glow.

I could make out the movement of the water as it flowed past the house. Then I felt a strange sensation. I wasn't alone. The hairs on my neck stood up. In the white mist up over the river, floating just above the rock where the baby was stuck, was Namgay, his eyes closed and legs crossed in full lotus position, naked, except for an orange shawl around his torso. His mouth formed the sounds of some mantra I couldn't hear over the noise of the water. I called his name and his body dropped into the river. I could see him just below the surface.

I couldn't go back to sleep.

That morning, I was on the riverbank by 6, watching the corpse still riding in the water. Namgay came up beside me.

"I thought everything was impermanent," I said. "This thing seems pretty permanent."

"It's really stuck," Namgay said.

"It has to go," I said. "I mean it." I was more upset than I realized; I started to cry. He looked at me and finally took pity on me.

"I'll go talk to the Indians," he said. "I don't know if they can help. In any case, we'll have to pay them."

"Let's give them all the money we have."

He laughed. "A few rupees will probably do."

He stood there for a moment, thinking or praying, looking up at the mountains. It was Saturday morning, and I was planning to go to the weekend market in Thimphu to get vegetables. I felt drained and weak from lack of sleep, and hauling vegetables around the dusty market was the last thing I wanted to do. But at least I could get out of the house. I went inside to get a shopping bag.

When I came out to the car moments later, Namgay was walking slowly down the road. About half a mile from our house, there's a little bridge that crosses the river.

I stood at the river's edge and watched. What was he going to do?

I spotted him again after he'd crossed the bridge. He was headed to the building site on the other side of the river, but he had to double back toward our house. Indian laborers—about a dozen of them—were chatting and singing as they worked. They were thin as skeletons, but strong and energetic, with leathery brown skin that showed through their loose clothing.

They had no electricity, thus no power tools or heavy equipment. These workers had even hand-hewed the massive wooden beams that supported the house. They mixed concrete, carved, sanded, bent lengths of rebar—all with their own muscles. They worked like ants, scurrying up and down bamboo ramps, hauling concrete, planing wooden planks all day long. After hours—instead of kicking back and relaxing in the grass outside their semipermanent huts beside the river, or sitting down to a nice meal, or going to the local canteen for a beer, which is what sane people do—rain or shine they played intense, sweaty games of cricket.

Compared to India, Bhutan was a good gig for them. They could make almost double their Indian salaries, that is, if they could find work at all in the depressed places they came from, like Bihar and West Bengal. Many of them made enough money building houses in Bhutan to send their children to private schools in India. They were master carpenters and craftsmen and had lived in Bhutan on and off for years.

I watched as Namgay walked up to one of them. I could see him talking, probably in Nepali, as he didn't know much Hindi. Everybody in this part of the world speaks Nepali. I could see the familiar way he stood. No matter to whom he was talking, his gestures and body language always conveyed an egalitarian respect.

To the Indian workers, he was an important man. I could see that the man was listening with his head down, his eyes probably off to the side, not looking straight at Namgay, in the Indian way of showing respect. Namgay gestured toward the river and then made a spinning motion with his arm. Several of the workers were listening to him now. The man he was talking to intermittently did the head wag peculiar to India.

As I stood on our side of the river in the yard I felt wildly impatient. It always took longer for things to be said in this part of the world. Namgay often repeats things or says the same thing in different ways when talking with Indians or Bhutanese. I think it's a way to be polite, a conversational dance—especially if he's trying to convince someone to do something.

Another man joined the conversation. He must have been chewing tobacco or doma, because he turned his head and spat frequently. The conversation didn't seem to be going Namgay's way. Five minutes went by, then ten. Once he gestured toward the house, and they all looked my way. I smiled, feeling stupid. But the Indians were used to the mysterious ways of white people, and maybe used to doing their inexplicable bidding.

Namgay and the eight Indian laborers began to move in my direction. They all walked quickly, purposefully, like a small army, toward the corpse. It was bloated now.

They arrived at a spot directly opposite the house; they were looking.

Way to go, Namgay, I thought. He had obviously convinced them to untangle the baby girl from the rocks. But how?

Overnight, monsoons had swollen the normally calm river, which a short person could wade across comfortably, to over eight feet high, and it was moving fast as it churned and eddied over the many rocks beneath the surface. It spilled water the color of chocolate milk far up on the banks.

The men gestured up the river, down the river, then talked again. Two of them defected and went back to the building site. The others kept talking. Sometimes their words and gestures seemed heated, especially Namgay's.

I soon realized that the other two hadn't defected. They came back with a very large coil of rope. Then they all began to disperse and take their positions.

Two of them took the rope and walked about 30 feet upstream to where a large tree on the bank bent toward the river. The tallest man wrapped one end of the rope around his waist, then tied it around his friend's waist a few feet down, and then lashed the other end to the tree. Then three more Indians came up near the tree. They were spaced maybe an arm's length apart, and they held each other's hands. What the hell were they doing?

The first man with the rope around his waist slowly eased himself into the river. Everyone yelled.

The tall Indian quickly disappeared in the murky water. I gasped. His friend on shore jerked the rope and the man's head appeared above water. Then two others sprung into action. They let go of each other's hands and grabbed the rope, further reinforcing the man in the water. If he drowned, at least they could retrieve the body, I reasoned. This was a very bad thought. I felt a wave of panic.

But he kept his head above water, held the rope, and managed to aim himself toward the rock with the baby stuck to it.

Then, without warning, his friend on shore leaped, and he was in the water too, splashing and flailing against the current with his spindly legs. He looked like he was trying to swim, but it was ineffectual against the strong current. Nonetheless, he held tight to the rope and kept his head above water.

What foolishness I had instigated. This little circus act was wildly dangerous. All it would take to knock one or both of them senseless was a big log careening down the river. Drowning was also a very real possibility. Then there would be more corpses in the river. "Get out get out get out," I said to no one.

Namgay had a piece of the rope now, too, as if to give moral support to the two in the water.

The first man got close to the baby. He made a few futile swipes with his arm to try to untangle the clothes. It didn't work. I was worried that the rope would break. The others on the bank must have had the same thought, because they began reeling the two men in the river back to the bank.

They looked like drowned rats as they climbed out of the water onto the bank, their wet clothes clinging to them. They sat on the grass catching their breath, coughing, and rubbing their heads and faces. But I could hear them laughing. This was sport for them.

After they sat a while, they untied the rope from

their waists. Two new men quickly stepped up and, merrily, tied the rope around their own thin waists. They were going to have a go at this game.

The second team was successful. The first man bobbed feet first straight to the rock where the baby was attached. He'd had the brilliant idea to bring a stick with him. A couple of hard jabs and the clothes were free. The baby's remains floated quickly down the river and around a bend.

When she disappeared, there was an enormous cry from the Indian men. I, too, yelled and clapped my hands above my head. "Waaa hoooo!" I screamed and danced.

The others quickly pulled the men from the river. There was a lot more yelling and laughing and back-slapping before they untied their friends and the tree. Then finally the head man coiled the rope and everyone walked back toward the building site.

Namgay waved to me across the river. Elated, I waved back. I felt infinite love and boundless compassion. Whatever happened, our karma together was good.

Where can I find a man who has forgotten words?
I'd like to have a word with him.

— CHUANG TZU

Thinking does not lead to truth.
Truth is the beginning of thought.

— HANNAH ARENDT

BLISS

One night a few months later, the call came. There was a six-year-old girl living in a remote village near Namgay's who needed help. She was bright and eager to learn, a little willful, but a good girl. Her walk through the mountain forests of Bhutan from home to school and back every day was almost four miles.

She would fall into bed when she came home, too tired to speak or eat. She couldn't have been learning anything at school. Did we know anyone who would adopt her? Bhutan is a developing country, poor by Western standards, and so it is common for friends or relatives who are better situated to formally or informally adopt children in need.

I'd met this girl on one of our trips to Trongsa. She was adorable, with a little round face and close-cropped hair. Her parents dressed her in boy's clothes, maybe a cousin's hand-me-downs. She wasn't shy; and, yes, she did appear to be a little unruly. That's what I liked about her. Her name was Kinlay.

Except there was a reason I'd reached middle age with no children. While the alarms on the biological

clocks of my friends back in the U.S. had gone off nois-
ily over the years, mine seemed to be inactive. Sometimes I pretended to anguish along with them. "Of
course, children give meaning to your life," I heard myself saying, but I didn't really mean it. Children were
only mildly interesting to me. I liked my friends' children and enjoyed watching them pass the watersheds
of potty training, kindergarten, elementary school,
adolescence, learning to drive, and so on, but it was
enough to be a semi-passive observer. Life was plenty
interesting, exotic, child-free, and insular, perfect for
lots of navel-gazing and hiking around Bhutan.

I thought I'd covered all the bases when Namgay
and I married. We discussed having children, and I told
him American women didn't usually have kids past 40
without taking fertility treatments. I had to make this
clear because Bhutanese women remain fertile—some of
them—into their 50s. It might be a function of diet, or
environment, or genes. I told him I was probably too old
to get pregnant.

"It's okay," he said, "We can have children in the
next life."

I liked having that deferment. The case was closed,
or so I thought.

So when the call came, we talked about it. Namgay
wanted Kinlay. I hemmed and hawed about what would
happen. It's always been hard for me to take the role of
the realist—because I'm not one. But often in our marriage I find myself doing just that. Secretly, I was worried
about what might happen if two Bhutanese nationals, a
man and a child, ganged up on a lone American woman.
And was Namgay thinking we would send her to col-
lege? Or take her to the U.S.? Or feed her three meals

a day? Or clothe and school her? What would we feed her? Where would we get a bed? Where would she go to school? Who would help her with her homework? I was putting up every roadblock I could dredge up from my limited knowledge of raising children. I had raised animals—dogs and cats. And that was a big commitment, let me tell you. It was no joke when they got sick, when they needed food or to go potty. Could Namgay and I take on a six-year-old child? What if she got sick? What if she had to go to the toilet?

"We can do it" was Namgay's answer to all of my questions, or "We'll manage."

I said we should wait and discuss it over a period of time. We didn't need to rush into anything. We talked until very late that night and then went to bed. I had to get up early the next morning and go with his cousin to visit her mother.

Cousin Pema is a small, lively woman in her 50s, but she looks and acts much younger. She has the bang-and-bob haircut—long ago it was called a "Buster Brown" or pageboy—that's standard issue for ladies of a certain age in Bhutan. Her brown eyes, large and wide, are always laughing, and her laugh sounds like singing. When she giggles, which is often, she puts her hand up to her mouth to be polite. She is well educated, but lives simply. She has a big party every June to celebrate Guru Rinpoche's birthday.

She wakes up at 5 A.M., before sunrise, washes her face, gets dressed, and starts cooking for the household. Her three-story house in Kawajangsa is large enough to accommodate her husband, four semigrown kids, and her ever-expanding heart.

In addition to her own family and occasionally her mother or one of her brothers, she also takes other people and their children. People who fall on hard times and have children they can't feed send them to Pema. Orphans with empty stomachs and broken hearts are also brought to her. She takes in women whose husbands beat them and run away with other women. Everyone knows she will never turn anyone away. They stay with Pema and her family for a while; and when they're ready, or when they get a little luck or a little money, they move on.

A few years ago, when Namgay and I lived in the house next door to Pema's, she had 11 children, including her own 4, ranging in age from 8 to 18 living with her. I'd wake up to see her beating rugs in the front yard at the crack of dawn. She is an absolute workhorse of a woman; and she looks like a young girl, with energy that comes from some divine source. She is the center that keeps everything around her going.

The house is noisy, chaotic, clean, and loving. The headquarters are in the kitchen where she fixes food, cleans, or holds court. We see her walking down to the market to buy food with a big, brightly colored plastic woven shopping bag, the kind that is ubiquitous in Bhutan, slung over her shoulder.

Occasionally she enlists me to be the driver or assistant on one of her missions, and going somewhere with Pema is always a good time. On this occasion, we were driving up to a pass near Ha and then walking a few hours into the pine forest to visit her mother, who lived in a meditation center. Pema wanted to take her some provisions.

Many people go into meditation when they are elderly. They become devotees of Chenrezig, the Buddha

208

of Compassion, and pray to him to help them get ready for their next reincarnation. Essentially, they are preparing to die and trying to improve their karma. But it isn't sad. It seems to give their lives a sense of purpose and keeps them fit and independent much longer than the elderly in other cultures. Many of them die while meditating, which is a very good thing in Buddhist belief. Everything in the body just slows down and then stops. It's very common in Bhutan to have out-of-the-way communities of devotees and older people. There is often a monk school, or *shedra,* in the vicinity where young boys and girls study to become monks and nuns. They help the old, and vice versa.

Pema's mother must have been in her 70s. She had raised seven children in the village and had worked, like most women of her generation, on the family's farm. Like Pema, she was energetic and very active. Everyone called her Angay, which means "grandmother" in Bhutan. Many older women are simply called Angay.

Occasionally Angay would come down to Thimphu for a few days to see her family and visit the Traditional Medicine Center above Pema's house to get herbal medicines for her aches and pains. In winter she'd organize a trip to Bodh Gaya in India, a favorite pilgrimage site for Buddhists, the place where Buddha attained enlightenment.

"Meditation center" is a misnomer, as there is no center there, only a few huts on the side of a remote mountain overlooking a beautiful alpine valley. If you look north on a clear day, you can see the imposing white peaks of the High Himalayas stretching into Tibet.

The family built a house there for Pema's mother. It is a small, neat structure of timber and pounded mud: wood and mud makes for good insulation, which she needs, because it's cold in the mountains. Namgay helped paint the outside. Her two small rooms are heated by an efficient woodstove. Two monk brothers who live and study nearby visit her daily to fetch her water from a garden tap, since there's no inside plumbing, and make sure she has enough wood to light her stove and stay warm. She cooks meals of rice and vegetable curry for them and gives them tea.

A garden surrounds the house. It is magnificent in the summer, with flowers and vegetables dense and fragrant in the Himalayan sun. Some of the flowers grow taller than the house and climb the fence that surrounds the yard. In summer you forget you're high up in the Himalayas in a remote retreat; it has the feel of a proper English garden.

Once we'd parked at the pass, we pulled out great packs of provisions, boxes, jars, and sacks to take to Angay and laid them on the grass next to the car to organize it all. This was the part I hated. I'm lazy about walking with a lot of weight strapped to my back; and Cousin Pema, ever munificent, pushes the envelope of what we, two lone women, can manage to haul up the side of a very steep mountain. She'd brought about ten pounds of recently harvested apples; ten pounds of red rice; 20 eggs packed in hay in a recycled bucket that had held oil for butter lamps; some momo, or meat dumplings, a local specialty for us to eat with Angay; three pounds of butter; another three pounds of locally made cheese called datse; a box of pastries from the Swiss Bakery; some dried beef, cut in strips; assorted onions, tomatoes, garlic, potatoes, long white radishes, and dried pumpkin; and, finally, a big jug of whey, the liquid that separates out of curdled milk. It's supposed to be rich in minerals and vitamins, but it looks like cloudy cow urine.

I glanced up at the mountain we were about to climb. Behind me, Pema expertly tied the meat, fruit, vegetables, and pastries onto my pack, leaving the heavier things for herself. Even so, I felt as if I'd fall over backward with the weight.

She outfitted her own pack and lifted it up over her back. I kept up a steady stream of admonitions, as required by Bhutanese protocol: "Give me the eggs. I can carry them in my hand." "Please." "You're carrying too much. Give me more." "My pack is much lighter than yours." "Please." "I'm much bigger than you. I can take more." But of course she wouldn't relinquish any of it.

Other times when we'd started off on a visit to Angay, we'd met a small monk or two at the trailhead and enlisted them to carry some of the food up the mountain. But today, bad luck; no monks appeared.

There was already some snow on the trail, but the day was warm. The trail would be a little muddy in places where the sun didn't shine. We had to look out for white monkeys who, it was reported, occasionally attacked lone monks walking along the trail and bit chunks out of their arms.

The first part of the trail was deceptively easy and even sloped downhill. We ambled along and passed three chortens and a prayer wheel making its *ting ting ting* sound as a small stream turned the wheel and rang the little bell. Then the trail aimed upward into denser forest.

Pema said we should make a lot of noise. "That won't be hard for the two of us," I said. She laughed her little song of a laugh. We, or rather she, kept up a steady stream of conversation, punctuated by a sentence or two from me as I huffed and puffed up the mountain.

Even with the big pack, I was glad to be walking. Hiking in Bhutan is my reason for living, and this is no exaggeration. I achieve a kind of euphoria: thin mountain air, brain chemicals, and brilliant sun. Bhutan is like a giant Stairmaster. The isolation and the mountains that surround us feed me. I've made peace with loneliness. "You gain some things and you lose some things" is the response Ken Kesey purportedly made to the question of how his life had been altered by numerous doses of LSD. I feel the same way about living in Bhutan. If you live for many years in this remoteness, you lose the ability to worry about small things and gain a penchant to be a little antisocial. I'm not a big fan of the human race, that is, the struggle to achieve. There's so much else to life. Living in isolation, you become fascinated with minutiae, but nothing is really of much urgency. Living in Bhutan has given me a vibrant inner life—and thigh muscles that can crack walnuts.

I started to break a sweat. Pema's brow was dry as a bone. She took pity on me; and every 20 minutes or so, we'd stop to breathe and take in the view. Pema filled me in about the comings and goings of the large, extended family of which we are a part. It's wonderful to be related to so many people. In our family there are clerks and judges in the High Court, politicians, teachers, painters, wood-carvers, filmmakers, and many monks and lamas, all industrious and devout. There's the occasional tragedy: an infant death, a student failing in school, an illness.

Very high in the mountains, we turned a bend in the trail and saw the house, and Angay's neat fenced-in yard. It was late fall, and there were a few potatoes and cabbages planted among the dead flowers. We found Pema's mother outside pulling massive sweet-pea vines off a trellis, and she greeted us warmly but kept working for a few minutes while we took the packs and our shoes off.

I could see the remains of canna, dianthus, and sweet peas, with an occasional faded bloom among the dried brown plants. Even with the vegetation dying back, the view from Angay's garden evoked Shangri-La. Distant mountains shrouded in clouds, partially obscuring golden-roofed temples off in the distance, days and days away, and so inaccessible you wonder how they were ever conceived and built. Perhaps I was dreaming—they might not exist at all. Everything at that altitude takes on an unreal quality as it shimmers in the sun.

We'd had no way to let Pema's mother know we were coming; but when she ushered us into the house, we found she had already started cooking a big meal for us. The day before, her nose had been itching, she said, laughing shyly. That meant she would have visitors, so she got up that morning and started to prepare.

We sat down in her kitchen next to the woodstove. A swath of bright sun came in through the huge picture window and cut across the floor. A gray cat with mangled ears had positioned itself just so on the thick wooden floor, curled in sleep with geometric precision to take full advantage of both the warmth of the stove and the shaft of sunlight. Like all cats in Bhutan, she was a working feline; she kept rodents out of the house. Angay fixed us tea and sat down with us while we drank. The cat abandoned her prime real estate to curl up in Angay's lap as she sat cross-legged on the floor. Angay stroked her absently as she chatted with Pema.

We spent all day in the kitchen by the stove and went to bed when it was dark, making pallets on the floor from giant Chinese blankets with pandas on them bought from the nearby Tibetan border.

I woke in the middle of the night and heard Angay reading scripture out loud in her tiny bedroom, which also served as the temple room. It had a small altar and several gold statues and the obligatory seven bowls of water. She slept on the floor in front of the altar. Now, the dim light of a lone bulb cast her shadow on the wall as she rocked slowly back and forth and chanted, taking long, deep breaths in between the phrases. It must have been 3 or 4 A.M. The cadence lulled me. Lying there in the old woman's hermitage gave me the most profound sense of calm I've ever felt.

The next day, we folded our bedding, ate a little rice for breakfast, and hiked up to a sacred place where "holy water" flows out the side of a mountain. The spring was one of many in Bhutan created by Guru Rinpoche when he threw his staff down into the earth. He was always doing magic with the stick: wherever I went in Bhutan, people pointed out little rivulets or springs that were created by Guru's magic. There were also footprints or handprints he'd left behind in rocks. Manifesting or planting apple trees was also a popular activity. Sometimes he'd throw his stick down like a spear and an apple tree would sprout up; sometimes he used the more traditional method of planting seeds.

Angay asked Pema if it was true that Guru Rinpoche had reincarnated and was living in a place called "Sweezer-lan."

"Switzerland?" Pema asked. "Who told you that?"

Angay smiled and didn't say anything.

Pema looked at me and grinned. "Maybe," she said.

"I heard he was living in the Bahamas," I said, joking.

I washed my face in the holy water and prayed for enlightenment. If that was too ambitious, I asked whoever was listening for a large sum of money. Again, whoever was listening could decide whether or not it was an appropriate request. I was, after all, living in Bhutan, where greed and accumulation of wealth wasn't a big issue. Although I've never been poorer in my life than I am now, I've never felt more secure or happy. Nobody starves in Bhutan. I didn't make a prayer about Kinlay, although she had been on my mind a great deal during our visit. My thoughts were focusing on one question: could I be a mother?

Walking down the mountain on the way back to Thimphu, Pema talked rapid-fire, but now I could keep up my end of the conversation because we were going downhill with nothing in our packs.

"Would you ever go for retreat, like your mother?" I asked her.

"Who knows?" she answered.

After a while we stopped to rest on an old log beside the trail.

She talked about some friends who had begun to pray and meditate as they grew older. "They're always going on a pilgrimage, to this temple or that temple. They pray every morning and every night," she said.

I couldn't tell what she thought about these habits of prayer and purgation.

"Do you meditate?" I asked her.

"Look at where we are," she said, getting up from the log and not answering my question. "I love to talk when I walk," she said, moving on the trail. "Then I get to a place and I think, *I'm already here. How did that happen?*"

Her evasion told me the question wasn't necessary. It wasn't skillful. I didn't care about the answer. It wasn't even the question I wanted to ask. How did she know? What I really wanted to ask her is how she did it. How did she raise all those kids?

Long ago, on my first trip to Bhutan, in a strange, new place where everything was the opposite of what I expected, I asked and got answers to many questions. Sometimes when I asked a question, I was met with silence. But sometimes in the silence there were answers: *What does it matter when we get there? We are here now. How is it for you here? There probably won't be any hot water in your hotel room. The world is getting smaller. What each one of us thinks matters and our smallest actions affect everyone on the planet. There is no power in not seeing and in not being aware. Try to get out of yourself and overcome your ego. You might be a good mother. You might not. What good does it do to ask that question?*

In my life, adventure and dreams have taken precedence over desire for material objects. I follow my intuition and my dreams because this is the only way change happens. I'm not averse to working without a net. And I'm not averse to leaps of faith.

In the West, it is possible to live and be asleep. In Bhutan one is compelled to wake up. There are all kinds of ignorance in the world. Education, learning to read and write, doesn't necessarily give us knowledge. We have to learn to use our minds to see what is really happening.

In the midst of my pondering, it hit me like a thunderbolt: For every minute I mulled, probed, and questioned, Kinlay was struggling. Kinlay was up in the air. A child was suffering.

In the end, it was a no-brainer. I didn't let go of any

of my numerous doubts, but I followed my intuition. I said yes. I took the plunge into motherhood and vowed to be the best half-assed mother I could possibly be. It was 11th hour, seat-of-the-pants, last-minute motherhood, for which I was nominally prepared. I was hoping against hope that my long-dormant instincts would kick in and guide me.

And they have. Sort of.

Some things in life are more important than understanding.

EPILOGUE

As I write, I can hear Namgay painting in the room above me. Painting is usually a semi-silent endeavor, but not where we live. While he paints, he chants soft prayers to the deity whose image he's creating. He says this helps him paint better and gives the thanka power.

Namgay's prayers waft through the open window of the little sunporch where I work and make the hair on the back of my neck stand up as I write. I feel I am getting some residual good karma. Anyway, let's hope.

Namgay has a few gray hairs now, but he still looks young. He is still shy, but not with me. His work is slow, meticulous, and deliberate, and it can take months to complete one of his intricate paintings.

He paints with ancient Bhutanese methods, starting with simple cotton cloth that he stretches and sews with twine onto a wooden frame to make a canvas. He covers the cloth with a layer of gum and calcium chalk, then rubs it hard, first on one side, then on the other, with a river rock to make it smooth. He paints and rubs the canvas three or four times until it is perfect and will absorb the paint evenly without cracking. The word *thanka* means "rolled art," and so these paintings of Buddhist deities and other images are rolled and unrolled for hundreds of years. Most are kept rolled up and stored until holy days or ceremonies. Then they're unrolled and hung on the walls of temples. It is art that will live for many generations.

After preparing the canvas, Namgay draws an elaborate figure, a Buddhist god or goddess, in the Bhutanese style, with sky and earth in the background, and then begins to paint it with pigments he has made from crushed stones—lapis, malachite, vermilion—or minerals and plants, mixed with gum and water. Every thanka is painted in the same sequence: he paints the sky and earth, then the clouds, then the body of the deity, then finally the face. He'll only paint the face of a deity first thing in the morning, because then his hand is very steady and his mind less cluttered. It is important for the mind of the painter to be as pure as possible. The last elements to be painted are the eyes; and when the eyes are painted, the thanka is "awake."

Namgay's thankas are known for their precision and for the beautiful, serene faces of the deities. The figures he paints are prescribed by a tradition that goes back hundreds of years. My favorites are the *Neten Chudru*, or Sixteen Arhats, the students of the Buddha who took the dharma to the four corners of the earth. I like the *Dakini* he paints: beautiful enlightened women, attendants to the deities, ornamentally perched in clouds like angels, pouring oil and holy water down out of the sky. I also have a special feeling for Dorji Drolo, the wrathful manifestation of Padmasambhava, or Guru Rinpoche. He reminds me to fight for what I love and try to subdue my anger and ignorance.

Namgay can draw the figures perfectly, with just the right proportions. He learned the thousands of different positions of the Buddha, Green Tara, the God of Compassion, White Tara, and Dorje Sempa in school. For him, painting is a meditation, an act of piety.

The final step of painting a thanka is to highlight the flowers and leaves and the brocade and jewels of the figures with pure gold dust mixed, again, with gum and water. The gold is polished with a special stone, a long, thin agate, to make it shine. I love to watch this. The surface shimmers as Namgay's patient hand makes infinitesimal, deft strokes with the stone, and the gold comes alive. Rub too soft and the gold won't polish; rub too hard and the canvas will crease or tear.

The painting is a living jewel, every detail perfect. If he doesn't make the thanka perfect, he says, then the person who has commissioned the painting won't have a good reincarnation, and neither will he, the painter.

Namgay makes his own brushes from the summer hair inside cows' ears. This is particularly fine hair for the intricate designs and tiny, almost invisible lines: hair of the gods, tiny, perfect pink lotus hands, lines that capture breath and prayers. Our cat, who dines on canned sardines from India to make her fur oily and fine, supplies a slightly heavier grade of hair for brushes. Lately, I notice Namgay is branching out: several cats in our neighborhood have small chunks of hair snipped with scissors from their backs. He jokes that they are accruing merit, giving their hair to help make religious art.

Unlike Namgay, who is even and understated, I go up and down, and I talk a lot. I grew up far from anything or anybody Buddhist. Nevertheless, Namgay adores me. Now I understand that people come together sometimes for unexplainable reasons. Acceptance is so much a part of being in love, and love can make a person exceptional.

I came to Bhutan for the first time when I was 39. "A nice diversion" was how the travel agent put it. It was. Bhutan, the great distraction, has reshaped me until my life has become unrecognizable. I've lost 30 pounds, gained a Bhutanese family, quit smoking, started meditating, and learned to walk everywhere, and almost imperceptibly my ideas and attitudes have changed. I don't think it's wrong to work less, have less stuff, or go on more picnics. There's no moral here. It is possible that I've gone completely insane, but as the Bhutanese say when confronted with paradox, "What to do, la?" If I am going quietly crazy, I couldn't think of a nicer place to do it than Bhutan.

Of course, I'm probably not crazy, but after all these years, my sensibilities have been stretched and remolded; and I have come around to the Bhutanese way of doing things in many respects—eating, dressing, thinking, celebrating, praying, talking, laughing, having a casual attitude toward time. If I don't get it done in this life, then perhaps I will in the next.

I have found a voice and a home and a wonderful life among the people and mountains of Bhutan. I have learned to slow down, to pay attention, and to laugh. But sometimes I still need a wake-up call.

One day, about two years after we married, Namgay and I were sitting in our little garden behind our house beside the river. It was early morning and we had our tea, and we were enjoying the crisp June morning and talking about the flowers that were beginning to bud. I remembered I had some seeds in the storeroom that I wanted to plant, and I asked him if they would do better under the peach tree in the shade or beside the brick wall where they would get full sun. The conversation drifted. I can't recall the exact words, but it's what all married couples do—play remember when. Remember those flowers at the hotel in Lobesa? Remember when we ate at that restaurant? Remember when we went to Hawaii? Remember that man we met in Bumthang who we bought the sugar bowls from? Then Namgay said, "Remember that day I gave you a lift?"

"What do you mean?" I asked. "What lift?"

"On my motorcycle."

"You don't have a motorcycle."

"Before. That day you hurt your ankle."

"What?"

"In Punakha."

"What?! How did you know I sprained my ankle?"

"Because," he said sweetly and matter-of-factly, "I gave you a lift."

"No! That was you?" I jumped out of my chair. "THAT was you on the motorcycle?"

After so many years, the picture of the man on the bike was still vivid, that day when he rescued me on the road. The helmet visor obscured his features, except the lips. But I have certainly seen those lips since. *Of course.*

Talk about having the feeling you're on the right

track, or feeling like there's magic afoot. Why didn't he mention it before? I'm not sure. I ask him all the time. At different times, he says he forgot about it, or he just assumed I knew it was him—that I was in silent collusion. But now I know that's just the way he is. His equanimity and understatement are why I love him and why I love Bhutan, because to me they are inseparable.

I've learned not to question so much.

I understand that life is full of these happy, life-altering coincidences. They probably happen much more than we think or know, especially when we are traveling, loosed from our moorings, if you will. They happen quite often in Bhutan. And I know that if a day comes when you're in a place that seems absolutely magical, when you feel like anything can happen, you just have to go with it: go ahead and let yourself get carried away.

A LITTLE MORE ABOUT BHUTAN

Although progressive things are happening in Bhutan, many Bhutanese live much as their ancestors did, sowing the seven traditional grains in remote villages on the sides of steep mountains or in bowl-shaped valleys. Life is easygoing, made even easier by the Bhutanese propensity to take life slowly and laugh. Scotsman George Bogle, one of the first Westerners to visit Bhutan and fall in love with the place, wrote in his journal about the women of Bhutan in the 18th century, and what he said is still true: "The resources of a light heart and a sound constitution are infinite."[1]

The rules of social behavior in Bhutan are age-old. The ancient ways of conducting rituals and of caring for the environment and for each other, as well as the codes

[1] Clements R. Markham, ed., *Narratives of the Mission of George Bogle to Tibet and of the Journey of Thomas Manning to Lhasa* (New Delhi, India: Manjushri Publishing House, 1971), 65.

of behavior, manners, religion, and sensibility haven't changed all that much in millennia. Now suddenly, there's television, Internet, health care, cars, telephones, currency, roads, schools, and the opportunity to travel outside of Bhutan. These things have accelerated the transformation of Bhutan, and they have all arrived in less than one lifetime.

If I had to name the biggest difference between Bhutan and the rest of the world, I could do it in one word: *civility.* I hardly ever hear that word used anywhere else in the world.

It was certainly much in evidence when Portuguese missionaries came here in the 17th century. By all accounts, they enjoyed their stay but couldn't convert anybody with pictures of an Anglicized Jesus herding sheep; or dying on the cross; or as a fat, pink infant held by Mary. The Bhutanese strain of Tantric Buddhism, with its secret rituals, wrathful, flaming (as in on fire) deities, skulls, and phalluses, seems a better fit.

Within the small area that is Bhutan, there is every conceivable climate, from glacial in the north to temperate in the middle and rainy in the south. Bhutan is home to many endangered species of birds, flowers, and mammals, including monkeys, tigers, elephants, and rhinoceros. It is also home to blue sheep and snow leopards.

The mountains covering Bhutan grow and change shapes according to the weather and the time of day, the way clouds shift and make shadows along ridges, or the way the sun highlights a clump of trees. Clouds form around them or pour over their tops. This makes them seem alive.

The mountains become steep and impassable the farther north and east you go. Some people from eastern

Bhutan are small and squat, as if growing up in the shadows of the imposing mountains has stunted them. There's very little land to cultivate, as most of it goes straight up and down, though there are patches of cultivation between the crags and peaks. The road between Trashigang and Pemagatshel in the extreme southeast is suspended about three-fourths of the way up massive cone-shaped mountain peaks, and you look down at the sheer drop inches from the side of your car. A narrow river cuts through the gorge, but it looks like a thin line etched in the dust far below. It is not a hospitable place for people to live.

There are no roads in the High Himalayas where Bhutan meets Tibet. Some of the old yak herders say the mountains here are impassable. They describe the old days when they were young men and women and traded with the Tibetans. They hung ropes off cliffs and shimmied up and down from Bhutan into Tibet. When China invaded Tibet, they cut the ropes.

Geography has made it difficult to traverse the Himalayas, but improvements in road engineering in recent years mean that the Chinese have begun building roads at the border where Tibet meets Bhutan, and some of the roads have crossed into Bhutan's side of the map. The Bhutanese are worried.

There is no electricity in many villages in the east or in the remotest areas of the country, like the vast forests in the south and the glacial valleys of the north. The terrain makes building transformers for electricity and laying blacktop for roads difficult and expensive. In some places, heavy equipment must be carried on horseback or, where the horses can't go, by humans.

There are many meditation communities high up in the mountains. At one, a great three-story temple forms the center of the sanctuary, which sits on a flattened mountaintop. On the outlying mountainsides, a few small hovels and huts dot the landscape. There are many elderly practitioners and a few caretakers who wash and cook for the devout. The community numbers around 80 men and women and 20 student monks.

The young monks from the school run up and down this steep path because there is a tiny shop at the trail-head that sells apples in late summer. The kindly shop owner will never make a profit: he gives the apples to the young penniless monks.

The people of this community and their predecessors have lived in isolation for hundreds of years. But several years ago, the government, at great expense, gave them electricity, building poles to string the wires up the side of the mountain. Any other government would have simply told the people to come down off the mountain.

The area surrounding Bhutan is the geopolitical equivalent of a trailer park, full of fussing, warring tribes, pugilistic political entities, poverty, drugs, and religious opportunists, and it has a history of epic natural disasters. Climate change is making these natural disasters more numerous, and people talk about the possibility of "water wars" in the region if climate change continues at its current pace. China has swallowed or reclaimed (depending on your perspective) Tibet, directly to the north, and the Han Chinese are destroying what's left of Tibetan culture. South of Bhutan, where Assam and West Bengal meet, is the "Chicken's Neck," a piece of land about 40 miles wide, which connects the extreme northeast frontier of India with the rest of the country. Below the Chicken's Neck is Bangladesh. Its capital,

Dhaka, has the distinction of being the gun-running capital of the region and a center of Islamic extremism. It's also very poor, hot, and prone to natural disasters. Since 1949, not long after Indian independence, when Bangladesh formed—it was called East Pakistan then—it has never quite gotten on its feet. Much of the country is either at or below sea level, and it has more river deltas than any place in the world. During the rainy season the rivers swell, carry helpless villagers, cows, goats, and other livestock to their deaths, and overturn ferries packed with hundreds and hundreds of unfortunates, which occasions a five-second mention on the news crawl on CNN. Ever since George Harrison's Concert for Bangladesh in 1971, which he organized to raise money to help children caught between political and military upheavals and devastating floods, the name Bangladesh, if it doesn't draw a blank, evokes a nation of ill-fated brown people and babies with large, fly-encrusted eyes and swollen bellies.

On the upside, Bangladesh is a trading partner of Bhutan, so in Bhutan we all eat from the festive melamine bowls manufactured there, and the Bangladeshis, in turn, eat Bhutanese apples. We also wear "seconds"—defective Old Navy, George (a Walmart brand), Gap, H&M, Tara, and other lesser-known labeled clothing manufactured there, bought in bulk, and shipped to Bhutan by enterprising merchants. You might even be wearing something made by the women and children of Bangladesh.

Nepal, just one country over to the west, has had over 50 years of unstable, corrupt governments and has recently been taken over by Maoists, its king forced to leave. The once prosperous ancient Himalayan monarchy has suffered greatly from rich, unscrupulous landholders selling off its once abundant natural resources, such as lumber and minerals, and shamelessly exploiting its people. Tourism and foreign aid are the biggest contributors to the national coffers, which is not a sustainable situation. Even the once-exquisite Hindu and Buddhist temples have been carted away piece by piece by thieves. Members of Nepal's ruling families have not once but twice slaughtered each other—first during the 1846 Kot Massacre and again in June 2001. The Nepali people, who are mostly Hindu, have been terribly misled by their leaders and by unscrupulous journalists, and their country is in shambles. Some families sell their daughters to brothels in Mumbai, Calcutta, and Siliguri to feed the rest of their children. They are absolutely desperate, and Nepali refugees flood Northeast India and Bhutan. Now many who migrated to and were kicked out of Bhutan, along with other Nepalese, are starting new lives in the U.S. It is said that Nepal bleeds over a million people every year. This puts great hardships not only on the hapless Nepalese, but also on their neighbors, as the Nepalese now want to claim parts of India and Bhutan as their own.

There are parts of Nepal that look eerily like moonscapes; the vegetation and topsoil has been stripped and nothing can grow there. The Maoists have waged over ten years of civil war, ending the tenuous hold the greedy King of Nepal had over his subjects. Now they seek legitimacy and expansion of their power. But they aren't much better than their predecessors; and they have invoked draconian measures concerning marriage and property ownership, among other things. Money sent back to the country by friends and family who have left keeps Nepal's head above water, as is the case in much of the undeveloped world. These people have settled in places like Thailand, Hong Kong, and the U.S., and they support houses full of relatives back home. Many have gone to the Middle East, to countries like Qatar, to work in construction. Their lives are only worth as much as they can send home.

A military junta rules Burma, or Myanmar, to the east. In this beautiful, undeveloped country, the people are, as in Bhutan, Buddhist farmers. Burma is like the house in your neighborhood that you never see anyone going into or coming out of, but you suspect there might be bad things going on inside. This was especially true in the aftermath of a terrible cyclone that decimated the Irrawaddy Delta region of the country in 2008. But we can only imagine how much its people are suffering. Bhutan tends its own garden and doesn't meddle in the affairs of its neighbors. How could it? It is only a speck on the world map.

As China looms to the north, Bhutan's southern neighbor, India, is perhaps the less aggressive of the two nearby leviathans. Along the very porous border with Bhutan, it is said there are over 500 separate tribal entities and political groups with different agendas and manifestos, wanting to secede from the Indian states of Assam, West Bengal, Sikkim, and Arunachal Pradesh. In case you think you misread that, you didn't. That's a lot of people, about 15 million of them, all vying for a very small area of the world.

Assam, West Bengal, Manipur, Meghalaya, Arunachal Pradesh, Mizoram, Nagaland, and Tripura, the northeastern states of India, are places of extreme unrest. Every week a train station is bombed or some unfortunate local official who forgot his weekly tithe to the ULFA, the most powerful of the rebel groups, is found floating in a rice paddy. "The Centre," the nickname for the central government of India, rules from New Delhi, quietly attempting to keep the status quo. It's an old story: multinational corporations, aided by The Centre, drain tea, oil, and minerals from the natural resource-rich region. The northeast Indian state of Assam is said to have over 1.3 billion tons of oil reserves.

For about 200 years, up until the beginning of the 20th century, Tibetans often invaded Bhutan. The lush, sheltered mountain valleys, where anything could grow, tempted the Tibetans, since nothing grew on the cold high plateau they inhabited. When an invasion was imminent, the Bhutanese dropped their ploughshares and took up their bows and poisoned arrows and retreated to the nearest forest or fortress.

The Bhutanese had a lot to lose, so they were formidable opponents. I do not recommend you make a Bhutanese mad to see for yourself. Trust me when I say the Bhutanese are fierce. I mean flay-you-alive ferocious. Civility only goes so far.

The Tibetans were finally defeated and driven back at a place near Paro called Drukyl Dzong at the end of the 19th century. Ironically, when the Chinese invaded Tibet in 1959, many Tibetans were allowed to come and live in Bhutan as refugees. Large Tibetan communities still exist in Thimphu, Gidacome, and Bumthang, among other places.

Bhutan was never colonized, but while the United States was fighting its civil war, Bhutan was fighting for control of the Duars, the fertile river deltas in the south, which were semicontrolled by British India. The

Bhutanese lost the Duar War against the better-equipped and more numerous British and lost most of their flat land to the south. The British then ceded this land to India. My Bhutanese friends say they were pushed up into the mountains that nobody else wanted.

Given the neighborhood and Bhutan's small size—it's 100 miles from north to south and 200 miles from east to west—it's been in the country's best interest to lay low while the rest of the world rips itself to shreds. Only within the last 40 years has the country taken measures to end its isolation and take its place among the nations of the world. The Bhutanese did this both to modernize and to protect themselves: a country with a higher profile might be less likely to be swallowed up. The region is full of countries—Mustang, Ladakh, Sikkim—that were once Buddhist monarchies but are now part of India or Nepal. Bhutan is the last one.

Bhutan operated as a sort of medieval state until the late 1950s and early 1960s. Three successive kings of the Wangchuck Dynasty, which was founded in 1908, ruled Bhutan until then. All were benevolent despots to one degree or another. The third king, Jigme Dorji Wangchuck, perhaps feeling the hot breath of the Chinese at his door (China and India were fighting the Sino-Indian War, a border war, until 1962), began to modernize the country in earnest. For better or worse, he married his country to India, and with the help of his new ally, Prime Minister Jawaharlal Nehru, he began to build roads, hospitals, and schools and set a path of modernization that continues today. He joined the UN and formulated a political strategy with the ultimate goal of moving the country to democracy, eventually making himself and his progeny obsolete.

Bhutan has had its share of internal strife. From its earliest history, Bhutan was divided into different groups that frequently fought against each other. The mountainous terrain was helpful in keeping Bhutan isolated and allowing it to develop its distinct culture over the centuries. But it was not helpful in promoting solidarity. The Bhutanese fought among themselves and with Tibet, until they got lucky.

In 1627, luck came in the form of a high holy man from Ralung in Tibet, fleeing a dispute about his legitimacy. He came to visit friends and family and lay low for a while. His name was Ngawang Namgyal. He was one of the best things ever to happen to Bhutan.

Ngawang Namgyal is always portrayed in paintings and sculpture as fat and jolly with a long, Santa-Claus-style beard; but in truth he had a short, trimmed beard, and he wasn't fat. He was a military strategist, an accomplished Tantric master, a choreographer, an artist, and a brilliant mediator. He unified the warring factions in Bhutan, formed a dual government of secular and religious interests, forged alliances, and drove the warring Tibetans out of Bhutan once and for all. Under his rule, Bhutan became a single country, with a strong Buddhist culture. In his spare time, he did magic: Tantric, supernatural, unexplained enchantment. Every schoolchild knows stories about Shabdrung, as he came to be called, and his amazing feats. He could fly, for starters, and he could destroy his enemies with unexplained weather formations.

He started the *Zorig Chusum,* or Thirteen Arts, of Bhutan, an art school specializing in wood carving, painting, sword making, and other indigenous arts, which is still active today. Shabdrung understood the importance

234

of culture in shaping the lives and attitudes of people and in bringing them together. Because he was such a powerful man and a great leader and had no successor, his death was kept secret. After he died, his attendants brought food to the room where he was said to be meditating every day for over 30 years.

Traditionally a Buddhist monarchy, Bhutan is ruled by the fifth *Druk Gyalpo,* the hereditary King of Bhutan, Jigme Khesar Namgyal Wangchuck. He succeeded his father, who abdicated in December 2006. The country has recently evolved to become a parliamentary democracy, with a constitution and voting. True to form, the Bhutanese aren't taking the road most traveled to democracy. They held elections, ran for office, and moved the country to one person, one vote, but not because they wanted to—because their beloved king asked them to. They have a lot to lose if things go south: it's one of the few countries in the world that gives its people free health care and free education.

We should never underestimate the Bhutanese resolve. They have dodged major bullets, both literal and geopolitical, in their unique and varied history. Bhutan has survived by enlightened governance, by grace, by work, by luck, and by shear will. The country doesn't particularly need the rest of the world. But the world needs Bhutan.

GLOSSARY

angay – A grandmother, or an older woman.

ara – A locally brewed wine made of excess grains (wheat, barley, rye). Where I come from it's called moonshine.

Bailey bridge – A prefab steel-paneled bridge designed about 50 years ago by the British Army Corps of Engineers. These bridges have become indispensable in Bhutan, where mountain roads often get washed away. The Bailey bridges are easy and quick to assemble, without heavy equipment, and their parts are interchangeable. They can be trucked to an area in modular pieces and assembled there, and they are solid enough to withstand heavy usage.

cabze – A biscuit of fried dough made for ceremonies.

chappel – A rubber house shoe, otherwise known as a thong or flip-flop.

chipon – A gatekeeper.

chorten – A mound-shaped repository for relics. See also *stupa*.

choshom – An altar in a temple. Every Bhutanese household has one.

chu or sometimes *chuu* – A river. Mo Chu and Po Chu—*mo* means "mother"; *po* means "father"—are the Mother and Father Rivers, which begin above Gasa and flow through Punakha and down into the Indian Duars.

dasho – Boss or "sir." *Dasho* is a term of respect, as is the honorific *la,* as in "How are you, la?" A Bhutanese friend joked, "Use 'la' when you want to ask a favor of someone."

doma – Another name for areca, or betel nut, the mildly stimulating nut that Bhutanese people like to chew with lime and betel leaf.

dopchu – Bracelet. Not to be confused with *uzen,* or principal (not that you would do that).

driglam namzha – Manners. Basic rules for behavior in Bhutan that were formulated by Shabdrung Ngawang Namgyal, the great unifier of Bhutan, in the 17th century. Driglam namzha includes everything from dress to architecture to giving gifts.

Druk Air – The Bhutanese national airline. It's still the only consistent way to get to Bhutan.

dzong – A government and religious center. There are 19 dzongs throughout Bhutan. They were traditionally used as fortresses when warring tribes and the Tibetans invaded. They have secret tunnels and hidden water supplies and are large enough to house thousands of people for many years.

Dzongkha – The national language of Bhutan. Dzongkha actually means "language of the dzong," so in olden times it was the language spoken in the dzongs, the official language.

The Indo-Burmese valleys of Bhutan, India, and Burma are some of the richest linguistic areas in the world. There are over 300 separate languages and thousands of dialects in this region. Because of this diversity, an official, common language was needed.

ema datse – The national dish of Bhutan. *Ema* means "chilies" and *datse* means "cheese." It's served with rice and is very spicy and hot.

gho – The national dress worn by Bhutanese men. It crosses in the front like a bathrobe, and then the excess fabric is gathered at the waist and tied with a belt.

gup – A mayor.

Guru Rinpoche – An Indian saint, Padmasambhava, who brought Buddhism to Bhutan in the 8th century. He is highly revered in Bhutan. *Guru Rinpoche* is an honorific that means something like "precious lama and teacher." Also known as Guru Singye, he has eight different manifestations.

hemchu – A chest-level pocket formed by folds in ghos and kiras.

Je Khenpo – The spiritual leader of Bhutan.

kabney – A ceremonial scarf worn by Bhutanese men when they go to a temple, dzong, or government center.

kata – A white silk scarf given as a token of good luck or congratulations at births, marriages, promotions, etc. It's the Bhutanese equivalent of a Hallmark card.

kera – A long, woven belt that is wrapped around the waist to secure a gho or kira. Also a language in southwest Chad, but you don't need to know that.

kichu – A big, all-purpose knife, like a machete.

kira – The national dress for women in Bhutan. It's a rectangle about five feet by eight feet that's wrapped around the body, held together with a clasp or a brooch at each shoulder, and cinched at the waist with a belt.

koma – A brooch used to gather the kira at the shoulder.

Kuertop – Someone from Kuertoe, a region in the extreme northeastern part of Bhutan.

lhakhang – A temple.

lopen – Honorific term for teacher or "sir."

lyonpo – A minister in Bhutan. *Lyonpo* is an honorific term that's something like the British knighthood. *Lyonchen* is the title for the prime minister.

naga – A spirit that lives in the earth. Bhutanese try to appease naga because they can cause disease or illness if they are made unhappy. Naga hate pollution, and skin diseases are a favorite form of retribution they use to punish people who make them angry. They are depicted as snakes, and sometimes they have a woman's head and torso.

ngultrum – Bhutanese currency. It's tied to, and is the same monetary value as, the Indian rupee.

puja – A ceremony. It usually involves monks or nuns chanting, the blowing of horns, and lots of food and drink. Nearly every household in Bhutan has a yearly puja during the Losar, or New Year. Pujas can be performed for weddings, to pray for good health, for death or cremation, as consecration rituals, or at births. *Puja* isn't actually a Bhutanese word—it's Hindi—but most people in Bhutan use it. The equivalent word for a ceremony in Dzongkha is *rimdo*.

Punakha – A valley in western Bhutan, formerly the seat of government. Its temperate climate makes for excellent farming.

rachu – A ceremonial scarf worn by Bhutanese women when they go to a temple, dzong, or government center. It's usually woven from red silk or cotton, or it is embroidered with flowers or auspicious symbols.

samsara – This lifetime. In Buddhist philosophy, the world is made up of endless cycles of birth, death, and rebirth for all sentient beings. One cycle is a samsara.

Selj'e Sumcu – The Bhutanese alphabet of 30 letters. The alphabet is actually borrowed from Chöke, the Tibetan alphabet used for scriptures.

shedra – A monk school.

stupa – A mound-shaped repository for relics. See also *chorten*.

Tantric – The form of Mahayana Buddhism practiced in Bhutan. The word *tantric* or *tantra* is related to "weaving," and people who practice believe in ancient secret rituals to harness divine energy and make it possible to achieve enlightenment in one lifetime.

tdego – A short jacket worn by Bhutanese women over the kira. Just to confuse you, the unstructured, usually white cotton undershirt worn by men under their ghos is also called a tdego.

terton – A treasure finder. In ancient times, holy men who traveled in Bhutan and Tibet hid treasures—ancient religious texts, priceless religious objects such as statues, and other precious things. Tertons found the treasures that were revealed to them in religious texts or in their dreams, sometimes centuries after they had been hidden.

thanka (also tangka, thangka) – A painting or embroidery. *Thanka* means "rolled art," so the painting or embroidery is made to be rolled and unrolled, to be carried on pilgrimage or to be opened during rituals or celebrations.

Thimphu – The capital of Bhutan.

thrimpon – A judge.

torma – Sculpted dough made out of butter and flour, dyed different colors, and shaped into flowers or other iconography. The sculptures look like miniature totem poles and are placed on the choshom, or altar, during rituals.

uzen – Principal of a school.

wanju – A thin undershirt worn under a lady's kira, usually made of silk or polyester.

Zangtopelri – Guru Rinpoche's heavenly abode.

ACKNOWLEDGMENTS

Ben and Janine Cundiff and Joe and Judy Barker have been extraordinarily kind to Namgay and me and have made so many things possible. We are eternally grateful. Perhaps with the passage of time, they will be able to forgive us the 38 inches of snow and the long, dark night at 3,750 meters on Thrumsingla Pass; the accommodations from Hell in Samdrup Jonkhar; and the military escort that kept a loaded gun pointed at their heads all the way to Guwahati. Good times.

Thanks to Carol and Rob Stein, who, in 1989, showed me the little speck on the map that is Bhutan and pointed me in the general direction. I also have deep and abiding gratitude to Marie Brown and Bhutan Travel. Until I came along, she had a perfect record of clients returning from their vacations.

Thank you to my agent, the rare and wonderful Laurie Abkemeier. Thank you to my editor Patty Gift; as well as Sally Mason, Laura Koch, and Amy Gingery at Hay House. Special thanks to Anne Barthel, for fact checking things that aren't fact-checkable.

To all of my Bhutanese friends and teachers, including Louise Dorji, Ambassador Lhatu Wangchuk (the first Bhutanese I met), Aum Dago Beda, Dawa Lhamo, Geydun Pelzang, Ugyen Zam, and Ashi Khendum, thank you for your inspiration and help. Thank you to Dasho Karma Ura and all of the researchers at the Centre for Bhutan Studies, especially for information about Chendebji, Trongsa. And special thanks to my guru, Thinley Dorji.

Also thanks to BJ Robbins, Jane Cavolina, Richard Loller, and wonderful Sherry Loller, who knew all along what was right. Thanks and love to Sarah Forbes and Roger Redpath, who are always in our hearts. The washing machine still works.

Last, thank you to Namgay, who is even more remarkable than I describe.

ABOUT THE AUTHOR

 **Linda Leaming** is a writer whose work has appeared in *Ladies' Home Journal, Mandala, The Guardian, A Woman's Asia* (Travelers' Tales, 2005), and many other publications. Eric Weiner included her in his 2008 bestseller, *The Geography of Bliss.* She has an M.F.A. in fiction from the University of Arizona; and she regularly speaks about Bhutan at colleges, churches, seminars, and book groups. She blogs regularly at www.marriedtobhutan.com and www.twitter.com/lindaleaming.

www.marriedtobhutan.com

READING GROUP GUIDE

1. Linda Leaming writes: "We all need a little Bhutan in our lives." However, she doesn't mean that we literally need to visit Bhutan. So what does she mean? Do you have things in your life that you're passionate about? What are they? How do you think Leaming was changed by Bhutan?

2. The Bhutanese have a different way of thinking about time. Is their view of time different from ours? What does it mean to think about time "cyclically" as opposed to "lineally"? How does their way of thinking influence their daily lives? How would it impact your own life?

3. Leaming says that in Bhutan "myth," "fact," and "fiction" have little meaning.

They have different ideas about what is real and illusory. What would it be like to live in a place where magic is thought of as an everyday occurrence?

4. Discuss the importance of fate, destiny, and reincarnation in *Married to Bhutan*.

5. Living conditions in Bhutan can be difficult for foreigners, with very few modern conveniences and comforts of the Western world. How do you think your life would be different with less? What could you live without? What are the things you feel you must have to live?

6. What are the differences between where you live and Bhutan? Talk about where you get your food, where you live, where you work, how you travel, and who you know. How are these different from what Leaming experiences in Bhutan?

7. "You find things when you're looking hard for other things. The trick is to be awake—which, granted, is harder than it seems. A sense of humor helps, as well as a willingness to accept whatever comes along—good, bad, or ferociously, violently different." Do you agree or disagree? What does Leaming mean by being awake?

8. Why do you think the story of Baje was included in the book? Do you identify with Baje?

9. What do you think about the stories of Drukpa Kunley? Do you believe using humor is an effective way to teach?

10. Leaming says, "Acceptance is so much a part of being in love, and love can make a person exceptional." Do you agree? How do you think this relates to her marriage to Namgay?

11. What does Leaming mean by the last line in the book: "Some things in life are more important than understanding"? Do you agree?

Hay House Titles of Related Interest

YOU CAN HEAL YOUR LIFE, the movie,
starring Louise L. Hay & Friends
(available as a 1-DVD program
and an expanded 2-DVD set)
Watch the trailer at: **www.LouiseHayMovie.com**

THE SHIFT, the movie,
starring Dr. Wayne W. Dyer
(available as a 1-DVD program
and an expanded 2-DVD set)
Watch the trailer at: **www.DyerMovie.com**

*COMMIT TO SIT: Tools for Cultivating a Meditation
Practice from the Pages of* Tricycle: The Buddhist Review,
edited by Joan Duncan Oliver

ELIMINATING STRESS, FINDING INNER PEACE,
by Brian L. Weiss, M.D.

WHY MEDITATE?: Working with Thoughts and Emotions,
by Matthieu Ricard

*WIRED FOR JOY: A Revolutionary Method for Creating
Happiness from Within,* by Laurel Mellin

All of the above are available at your local bookstore,
or may be ordered by contacting Hay House (see next page).

We hope you enjoyed this Hay House book.
If you would like to receive a free catalogue featuring additional
Hay House books and products, or if you would like information
about the Hay Foundation, please contact:

Hay House UK Ltd
292B Kensal Road • London W10 5BE
Tel: (44) 20 8962 1230; Fax: (44) 20 8962 1239
www.hayhouse.co.uk

***

Published and distributed in the United States of America by:
Hay House, Inc. • PO Box 5100 • Carlsbad, CA 92018-5100
Tel: (1) 760 431 7695 or (1) 800 654 5126;
Fax: (1) 760 431 6948 or (1) 800 650 5115
www.hayhouse.com

***

Published and distributed in Australia by:
Hay House Australia Ltd • 18/36 Ralph Street • Alexandria, NSW 2015
Tel: (61) 2 9669 4299, Fax: (61) 2 9669 4144
www.hayhouse.com.au

***

Published and distributed in the Republic of South Africa by:
Hay House SA (Pty) Ltd • PO Box 990 • Witkoppen 2068
Tel/Fax: (27) 11 467 8904
www.hayhouse.co.za

***

Published and distributed in India by:
Hay House Publishers India • Muskaan Complex • Plot No.3
B-2• Vasant Kunj • New Delhi - 110 070
Tel: (91) 11 41761620; Fax: (91) 11 41761630
www.hayhouse.co.in

***

Distributed in Canada by:
Raincoast • 9050 Shaughnessy St • Vancouver, BC V6P 6E5
Tel: (1) 604 323 7100
Fax: (1) 604 323 2600

***

Sign up via the Hay House UK website to receive the Hay House
online newsletter and stay informed about what's going on with your
favourite authors. You'll receive bimonthly announcements
about discounts and offers, special events, product highlights,
free excerpts, giveaways, and more!
www.hayhouse.co.uk